Home Outside

Home Outside

Creating the Landscape You Love

Julie Moir Messervy

The Taunton Press

 The Taunton Press
Inspiration for hands-on living®

The Taunton Press, Inc.,

63 South Main Street, PO Box 5506,

Newtown, CT 06470-5506

e-mail: tp@taunton.com

Editor: Peter Chapman

Copy Editor: Diane Sinitsky

Indexer: Lynne Lipkind

Interior design: Chika Azuma

Illustrator: Bethany Gracia

Photographer: Randy O'Rourke, except where noted

Library of Congress Cataloging-in-Publication Data

Messervy, Julie Moir.

   Home outside : creating the landscape you love / Julie Moir Messervy.

      p. cm.

   Includes bibliographical references and index.

   ISBN 978-1-60085-008-0 (alk. paper)

   1. Landscape design--North America. 2. Landscape design--Europe, Western. 3.

Outdoor living spaces--North America. 4. Outdoor living spaces--Europe, Western.

I. Title.

   SB472.45.M47 2009

   712'.6--dc22

                              2008032956

Printed in the United States of America

10 9 8 7 6 5 4 3 2 1

*To the people who have taught me the most about home:
my parents, William G. and Alice Butz Moir;
my children, Max, Lindsey, and Charlotte Messervy;
and my husband, Steve Jonas.*

Acknowledgments

I've enjoyed every moment of writing *Home Outside* because I've worked with such a talented team to make it happen. Peter Chapman, senior editor at The Taunton Press, brought his incisive and experienced eye to every detail of the book, traveling to my studio in Saxtons River, Vermont, many times to work with me and my team during its creation. Art director Alison Wilkes and photo editor Wendi Mijal shared their talents to ensure that the design and photography are as elegant but user-friendly as possible.

Mary Landon, publications manager at Julie Moir Messervy Design Studio (JMMDS.com), has worked tirelessly from the start in handling the call for submissions, organizing images, communicating with designers and photographers, and pulling everything together. Bethany Gracia, senior design associate, brought her outstanding design sensibilities to so many aspects of the book, especially in the illustrations and plans that add so much clarity throughout. Projects coordinator Kate Derwin, landscape architects Erica Bowman and the late Ed Hartranft, and landscape designer Jennifer Campbell have all contributed to the book at one point or another. I thank each of them for sharing their talents. Thanks also to my publicist, Suzanne Fedoruk, whose wise counsel has helped me at every turn. My husband and trusted advisor, Steve Jonas, continues to be my biggest supporter, caring for me in so many ways throughout the writing process.

Without the talents of many landscape designers and landscape architects from around the United States, Canada, and even Europe, this would not be the broad-ranging book of practical design ideas that it is. I thank you all, but especially Myke Hodgins, president of the Canadian Society of Landscape Architects, who helped us find a host of talented landscape professionals north of the border. A listing of all of the featured landscape professionals appears at the end of the book. Thanks also to the many photographers who provided images for us, especially Randy O'Rourke, who worked closely with me to photograph many of the properties. I also acknowledge photographers Nicola Browne, Ken Gutmaker, Genevieve Russell, and Allan Mandell. All of the photographers are credited at the back of the book as well. And perhaps most important, I thank the many homeowners from all around North America and Europe who agreed to have their properties photographed. I am so pleased that we can showcase such great talent in these pages.

Please go to our website, www.thehomeoutside.com, to find even more ideas, tools, and tips related to creating the landscape you love.

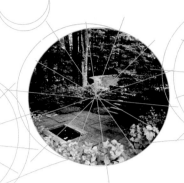

Contents

Introduction

Home is where the heart is. It's our sanctuary in a stressful world, the place we long to return to when we've been away. But home is more than just the four walls of our house; it encompasses the land around the house as well. When we turn down our street and pull into our driveway, we're home. When we open the garden gate, walk down the front path, and unlock the door, we're home. When we sit out on our deck, grill hot dogs on the barbecue, or play ball on the lawn, we're home. In many ways, our home outside is just as important to our sense of home as the inside is.

Yet most of us feel less confident about creating outdoor living spaces than we do about our interiors. Inside, we happily paint walls, choose finishes, and buy rugs, furniture, and fixtures, but when we step outside we're unsure of how to begin. That's where this book comes in. *Home Outside* is not just another garden- or landscape-design book. It's a step-by-step approach that lets you see your property through the eyes of a designer (that would be me).

For me, the home outside has been a place I've associated with pleasurable pursuits since an early age. Our family home was a small house on a one-acre lot in a Chicago suburb. At the end of a quiet lane, our house sat next to neighbors on one side and undeveloped forest on the other. My father kept most of the area as lawn so his six children could play softball with the neighborhood kids on summer evenings. My mother created two long planting beds set off by a pair of limestone walls and a large vegetable garden with a grape arbor to one side.

It was all pretty simple, but it worked well for us kids. No matter the season, we were outside all the time, riding bikes, climbing trees, making forts, or simply exploring the edges of the world my parents had created for us. In winter, my mother made us go out, no matter how bad the weather. When it was cold enough, we'd skate on the pond down the street or make igloos and angels in the snow.

As I grew up and left the nest, I kept being drawn back to my love of the landscape, eventually turning it into a career. For the past 30 years, I've helped homeowners transform their properties into the pleasure grounds they've always longed for. Through teaching and writing books, I've also given thousands of gardeners and landscape professionals the tools needed to design a home outside.

Strolling through your property is one of the best ways for you to get back to nature, to the garden that we all inhabit called Mother Earth. It's your own bit of ground where you can plunge your hands into the earth, watch the birds, view the night sky, or bask in the sun. It's the place where your children can view the world from atop a tree or hide within the shrubs, and where you can get physical by digging, pruning, or playing bocce or a quick game of touch football. It's your safe haven away from the world as well as a reminder of your responsibilities as one of our earth's stewards. As 19th-century writer Charles Dudley Warner wrote, when we have a bit of ground to call our own "... however small it is on the surface, it is four thousand miles deep; and that is a very handsome property."

Don't despair if your backyard looks like the photo above—just imagine the possibilities. With the addition of a terrace and some well-chosen plantings, this barren backyard landscape in Seattle was transformed into a treasured home outside.

A blank exterior wall is a good backdrop for displaying some of the things you love. Once you add some personal touches, you'll find it's a much more welcoming spot to sit.

A Pleasure Grou

One simple fact I've learned over my 30 years of practice is that people long for landscapes that bring them pleasure. They imagine enjoying a family meal on a terrace, napping on a hammock strung between two trees, floating on a raft in a backyard swimming pool, or clipping blossoms from a lovely flower border of their own design. Yet the truth is that there's little that's pleasurable about the typical American yard. The area around the house might include a shade tree and foundation plantings in the front and a deck and some grass in the back, but often there's little else to signal that the outside is used or enjoyed the way the inside is. Why is this? Why do we spend the bulk of our resources on the inside of our house, while settling for so little on the outside?

"I don't divide architecture, landscape, and gardening; to me they are one."

—LUIS BARRAGAN

Obstacles to Pleasure

There seem to be many reasons people ignore their outdoor surroundings. One is that we're all working longer hours as advances in technology enable us to keep connected wherever we are, including at home. This means less time for household chores, so many of us don't do the yard work our parents might have done, often hiring others to mow the lawn, prune the shrubs, or plant and mulch the garden. On top of this, family time has eroded with our complicated work schedules and after-school and sports programs that cut into the dinner hour, weekend leisure time, and even vacation getaways, allowing little time for the simple pleasures of outdoor family games or cookouts. Just as parents spend more and more time indoors, their children watch hours of television or play video games rather than spending time outdoors. The result: The home outside is neglected, unfinished, or forgotten in the rush to keep up with the pace of modern-day life.

(right) We all need a place where we can get away and feel close to nature. It doesn't have to be a teepee: A backyard swing or a bench under a tree works just as well.

(below) It's important to introduce the outside world to our children. Not only will they find pleasure in playing outdoors, but they'll also learn to love and protect nature as they grow older.

(far left) The typical American landscape consists of a house, driveway, front walk, and shade tree, all set upon a field of grass. There is little to encourage us to go outside where there's no place to be there.

(left) The small lots of this thoughtfully designed neighborhood development serve the residents' needs in two important ways. On a practical level, the individual lots are low maintenance, while on an aesthetic level, the delightful gardens feed the residents' spirits on a daily basis.

Developers and builders don't make homeowners' situations any easier. New developments in urban, suburban, and even rural areas around the country are being built on the little open land that's left, including meadows and forested areas, wetlands, and old farmland, all bulldozed to create cookie-cutter townhouses or huge houses on tiny lots. Trees are cut down, ledge blasted, and hills leveled to make the site-development costs more feasible. Ironically, by the time these developments are finished, all evidence of the original amenities for which they are named—such as "Oak Ledge" or "The Farm"—have been removed. Buyers are left with a fully finished house on a barren site that bakes in the sun, "complete" with a spindly tree, some tiny foundation plantings, and a few strips of sod. No wonder they feel demoralized.

In the suburbs, and increasingly in country settings, new "McMansions" have taken the place of older, smaller homes, dwarfing the lots and leaving little space for outdoor living or play. With increasing suburbanization, smaller lots, and less help available, many homeowners seek to create "no maintenance" landscapes for their property, with a sweeping lawn replacing garden beds and plantings pushed up to the foundation of the house.

What Will the Neighbors Think?

Neighbors and neighborhood associations can also damage a homeowner's morale. Strict rules about fence heights, paint colors, permissible plants, and maintenance schedules all help set a certain aesthetic standard for a neighborhood but don't necessarily promote personalization or novelty of design. Sometimes the critical eyes of those living nearby make us nervous about trying something new or different on the landscapes around our house.

DID YOU KNOW?

Research shows that children are smarter, better able to get along with others, healthier, and happier when they have regular opportunities for free and unstructured play outdoors.

LITTLE BY LITTLE: DEVELOPING YOUR PROPERTY OVER TIME

When landscape designer MJ McCabe started working on this Connecticut property, the only landscape elements present were a massive white oak, an ancient apple tree, two garden sheds, and a ragged walkway of slate that led from driveway to front door.

Every year, the designer and her clients tackled a new area of the site. They started by creating a brick front walkway, flanked with generous perennial borders of native (and wildlife-attracting) plants, including bayberry, aronia,

viburnum, and native cedars. The next year, they re-sided and painted their house and then, a few years later, built a family-room addition, resurfaced the driveway with peastone lined with granite cobblestone, and expanded the planting beds. This is the way that most of us create our landscape of home: little by little over time, making sure that each change works with the ones that came before it—and anticipating that it will work with any changes to come.

Over time, this modest Connecticut property was transformed into a landscape the owners could be proud of.

Neighbors and passersby are an important influence on your home outside. Think about creating a welcoming but usable front yard for all to enjoy.

Home and garden centers and landscape contractors, who may not always know the best practices or enjoy a fresh approach to design, often set the standards for landscape design. Many push the material on hand, choosing the standard concrete bench on the lot or a tree that hasn't sold, rather than specifying a style that goes with the house or the right plant for the right place.

On top of this, many of us move to a new house every few years, giving us little incentive to put effort (and money) into improving our property if we won't be there long enough to enjoy it. We do just enough to create "curb appeal" for the next buyer but don't spend the time or the resources to turn the outside of our house into a pleasure ground for ourselves and our family.

All this comes down to the fact that we feel more comfortable lavishing time and money on our house, rather than on our landscape. We feel the need to complete the roof over our head before turning our sights outward. There are plenty of books and magazines on creating individualized interior spaces—and on planting herb, woodland, or perennial gardens. But few publications explain how to organize and personalize the spaces around the house—how to turn them into home. While it's true that not everyone wants to spend the time it takes to maintain a beautiful garden, most of us would love to enjoy a welcoming front yard, a backyard that feels like an oasis, a place outside to entertain, a contemplative area, and a way to "flow" effortlessly throughout the house and landscape. The book you are reading will help you accomplish all this and more.

WHAT IS A PLEASURE GROUND?

The idea of a landscape as a "pleasure ground" is not new. From ancient times to the end of the 19th century, pleasure grounds were landscapes created in public or private settings as outdoor gardens for recreation, relaxation, and enjoyment. More then just planted places, these grounds offered different types of activities, from strolling to dancing to games such as chess and archery, and were dotted with ruins, statuary, fishponds, mazes, and pavillions in myriad styles—Chinese pagodas, Turkish tents, Moorish temples, and Swiss cottages. A public pleasure ground might include a zoo, an outdoor concert hall, a hunting park, or even an amusement park like the famous Tivoli Gardens in Copenhagen.

Sitting on a chaise longue under a spreading tree surrounded by soft plantings is heaven indeed.

Pleasure Principles

When you think about it, you can do pretty much anything you do inside your house, outside. You can cook, dine, lounge, play, and even sleep under the stars, but only if you create a home outside that works for you and your loved ones. To help you do this, I've developed a six-step process that hinges on six key principles. I like to call these "pleasure principles," given that the goal is to create a home outside that brings you pleasure. We'll look at each of the principles briefly here and then in much greater depth in the individual chapters of the book.

ACTUAL VS. IDEAL

Many of us live in houses with a bare minimum of landscaping—maybe a single tree and some foundation plantings.

Contrast that with the house (at right), where an added patio and mature plantings help give context to the house.

The Lay of the Land

To get an idea of the "lay of the land," you need to analyze your existing site and start to think about your ideal site. No matter how large or small and whether it's in a rural, suburban, or urban setting, your existing site is unique, but there are universal ways to understand it. By studying the conditions on your site, including the soils, sun, wind, slope, circulation, vegetation, and views, you'll have a clear picture of what you want to keep and what you want to change. From there, you can start to imagine your ideal site, bearing in mind the images, preferences, and ideas you already have about what you'd like to see happen on the land around your house. Part of the process is to complete a "designer's personality test" (see pp. 40–41) and to think about your aesthetic preferences, activity options, and favorite vantage points. When you're through, you'll know much more about what you already have and what you want your home outside to become.

(above) You are drawn to a certain property for a host of reasons. One attractive quality might be the slope of the land.

(below) The lay of the land affects the way your house sits on your property and how you actually experience it. Here, a handsome stone retaining wall accommodates a gentle change in grade.

(above) You need a set of organizing strategies to bring a sense of order to your property. Here, the owner designed a series of open-air rooms as her "big move."

(below) The big move here was choosing to plant around the foundation of this stately Victorian house, which is laid out as "house front and center."

Big Moves

The design process begins in earnest as you consider the "big moves" that you can use to organize the spaces around your house. You start by choosing one of four basic layouts: Immersed or Exposed, Central Clearing, House Front and Center, and Open-Air Rooms. In each of the layouts, the relationship between the house and the land around it is different. Then, you select an aesthetic arrangement: All Lined Up, Voluptuous Curves, or On the Angle. Used exclusively or in combination, these Arrangements help you make fundamental decisions about the kind of look you want on your property. Finally, you can identify a theme by determining a style, naming your property, or dreaming a "big idea" that pulls together your thinking about what you want your property to become. While not every property needs a theme, identifying one provides you with a clear vision for moving forward in the design process.

Comfort Zones

The design of different areas around your property affects your sense of comfort there. The Surrounding Zone is the area you live in—your region, town, or neighborhood that feels like home. Understanding its geologic makeup, history, and setting gives you context for the larger issues that affect your particular piece of land. The Welcoming Zone is the front face of your property, including the front yard, the driveway, and even your garage. It's an important zone because it's the one that says most about you to the people who pass by. In the Neighboring Zone, we look at the "enclosing arms" that surround your house and set you apart from your neighbors. Deciding how open or closed these enclosures should be and how they relate visually to your house is a critical part of the design process. Finally, we look at Living Zones to understand how to plan the amenities around the outside of your house. These include gathering, getaway, and play zones.

(above) Different zones around your house create a sense of comfort for you and your family. This courtyard garden is a "welcoming zone" for anyone who enters.

(left) How you design the enclosures around your yard depends on your relationship to your nearby neighbors. This tiny backyard feels both private and neighborly at the same time.

Flow occurs when you can move from place to place in an unbroken stream, with interesting pausing points along the way.

Making It Flow

The way you move through your property—how you make it flow—influences how you feel there. "Making It Flow" identifies three kinds of flow (moving, pausing, and stopping) and how they work together. It sounds straightforward, but there's a lot more involved than just putting down a path or a walkway. Part of making your landscape flow is providing places to pause, including gateways, landings, and turning points, and spaces to sit and enjoy the view. When things flow well, we are drawn outside onto our land and encouraged to move around it.

Placing the Pieces

While it might seem a relatively simple matter to position a birdbath, set a statue, or plant a rosebush, there are a number of basic spatial guidelines that will help you compose the elements of your property into a harmonious whole. "Placing the Pieces" entails conducting an energy audit to uncover positive and negative energy on your site. Using the "four Cs" (concentrating, connecting, conveying, and containing), you can place focal points on your property (the objects that stand out as the center of attention) and vertical and horizontal frames (structures that surround something that's special such as a focal point or a view).

(above) A hand-hewn birdbath peeks out over a verdant planting, an oasis for birds and a focal point for our eyes.

(right) Thoughtfully placing pieces that have meaning to us both inside and outside of our homes helps accent our surroundings.

Sensory Pleasures

You derive sensory pleasure by paying attention to the details of your home outside—from the scent of a rose to the sound of a backyard waterfall. These are the things that truly bring your home landscape to life. I've organized these finishing details by the elements of nature, starting with "Pleasures of the Earth," in which we look at the fundamentals of planting design, including trees, shrubs, perennials and annuals, and vegetable gardening. In "Water in the Landscape," we discuss designing water gardens and features. In "Fire," I talk about ways to find thermal delight and how to light your landscape. Finally, in "Air," I talk about air quality and well-being outdoors. Designing for sensory pleasure brings harmony and beauty to your home outside.

Bringing It Home

Ultimately, my goal with this book is to get people back outside onto their land by helping them realize the pleasure that's involved in being out of doors. I want to revive the home landscape as a place of importance in people's lives. By teaching you what I know about landscape design, I'm hoping that you'll learn how to create the spaces you love and go outdoors to enjoy them.

(top) The gentle sound of trickling water with a comfy chair nearby encourages us to stop for a relaxing moment between garden chores.

(above) Small spaces provide opportunities to create eye-catching compositions with a variety of colors and textures, as in this corner of a California dry landscape.

WORKING ON A SHOESTRING

Creating a home outside is a very personal statement that doesn't have to cost a lot of money. Garden designer Jan Enright was a self-employed single mother when she moved into her tiny 850-sq.-ft. mill house with her son 10 years ago. Working on a tight budget, she undertook all of the outdoor projects herself, using as many discarded materials as possible. The landscapes she created outside helped enlarge her tiny home, which she calls "Herbaceous Haven."

With the house situated on a pie-shaped lot with five adjoining properties, the immediate need was for some privacy screening, which Jan addressed by wiring bamboo screening on a roll onto her neighbor's chain-link fence. She used pot-bound plants that a nursery was discarding to soften the screen.

When Jan moved into her 50-year-old house, there were only three plants in the entire yard arranged along the

This little ranch house sits on a small lot overlooked by five close neighbors. After renovating the house, the owner started turning the barren yard into a garden sanctuary. The well-stocked deck makes a comfortable elevated perch above the lawn.

front foundation. She added some quick-growing trees for shade and beloved perennials dug up from her previous garden. She then divided the backyard into roomlike spaces using planting beds, which made the yard feel larger.

Today, even though Jan says she's "less broke," she is still hooked on the thrill of reclaiming objects for her garden. She recently scooped up a louvered front door with brass knocker, just like the one she grew up with, and attached it to her garden shed to hide the compost bin. She planted a 10-ft.-tall Greek column in the center of her newest shrub border, topped off with a queen fern spilling out of a low glazed ceramic pot. A firepit some friends were taking to the dump found a home at the edge of the stone patio. In a world of discards, Jan reuses found objects and makes them her own, continually crafting a very personal—and beautiful—home outside for herself and her family.

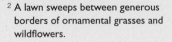 ¹Even the toolshed enjoys a garden at its feet. Jan gained privacy for her yard by using inexpensive cedar fencing and plantings.

² A lawn sweeps between generous borders of ornamental grasses and wildflowers.

³ This Shaker-style arbor acts as a seat, a gateway, and a frame for a birdbath beyond.

The Lay of the L

"*We are the children of our landscape;*
it dictates behavior and even thought in the
measure to which we are responsive to it."

—Lawrence Durrell

Remember the first time you set foot on your property? Most likely there was something about it that caught your attention, enough to part with thousands of dollars and a mortgage to be paid off over many years. You saw existing characteristics that you liked: the way the house sat on the land and related to its neighbors; the sunny backyard that was just the right size for outdoor games; the house's location in the city, the suburbs, or the country. You noted its special features: the flowering tree in the front yard; the handsome board fence around its perimeter; the large, open deck for entertaining.

You also saw potential for improvement. Perhaps you imagined adding a shade structure over the deck, planting a perennial border against the fence, or creating a rock garden at the front of the house. Subconsciously, you assessed the *actual* property—taking an inventory of the existing conditions—and envisioned your *ideal* landscape, mentally adding the features you've always dreamed of. This two-step process of weaving dream and reality is at the heart of creating your home outside. Let's begin by examining your actual site.

Your Actual Site

Taken together, your land, house, outbuildings, vegetation, orientation, and the soils that make up your property leave a unique imprint upon the earth. Studying these elements is a critical part of the process as you begin to think about designs for your property. The first thing you need to do is to conduct a site analysis in which you look at the many conditions that prevail around your yard.

To begin, you'll need a base plan to work from—a bird's-eye view of your property that shows the location of the house, the garage, property boundaries, and significant features of your landscape. Having a base plan enables you to mark the features that will stay and those that will change; it will serve as the foundation for all important decisions as you move through the design process. To get the most accurate base plan, you need to hire a surveyor. But if you live on a relatively level site that's not too large, you can create a working base plan yourself, as explained in the sidebar at right.

The planting beds along this typical suburban street veil views of passing cars and neighboring houses.

Most of us don't enjoy such an impressive vista, but even a close-in view adds interest. Make note of the features you like: the little woods at the edge of your land, the neighboring oak tree that hangs over your yard, or the simple bench that sits up against your garage.

Drawing in plan view isn't always easy, but it's well worth it. Rather than having to move heavy furniture, stones, or building materials around your property until they fit, you can move things around on paper first. Doing this also allows you to live with the way something will look before you actually build it. Drawing in plan view enables you to anticipate what problems might arise, such as how big the deck or patio should be to accommodate a grill and a picnic table. In addition, a bird's-eye view makes for one-stop shopping: You can give a fully worked-out plan to a landscape contractor and in return get an accurate price for the work involved. As we move through the design process outlined in the rest of this book, try out each of the ideas on tracing paper, keeping a "paper trail" of your drawings as you go. You'll find that you'll not only get more skilled at drawing plans but also become better at visualizing the final outcome of your designs.

Evaluating the Site

Once you've created the base plan, you're ready to begin the site evaluation, which you need to complete before moving forward with any design changes to your land. Start by noting all the reasons you fell in love with your property. These might include the size and style of your house, the way it sits on the land, the views, the neighborhood, the mature trees, or other special features. These are the *plus points* of your property—the elements you'll want to preserve no matter what else changes. Mark these assets with "+" marks on your plan.

Next, look for the drawbacks, or *negative points,* of your property: What are the problem areas you want to change? Perhaps you're too close to a noisy neighbor, or you can hear a dog barking incessantly down the street. Maybe you've bought into a new development and there are no trees left standing around your house. Or the builder placed the front walkway too close to the house. Or the first thing you see when you drive up is the garage door, not the house. Mark these drawbacks with a minus sign ("–") on your plan.

CREATING A BASE PLAN

Base plans are measured drawings that show the location of your property line, existing buildings, street and driveway, paths, walls, large trees, and, if possible, the grades at different points around your property.

To make your own base plan:

- Use a 50-ft. measuring tape to measure the dimensions of each side of your house.

- Measure the distance from each side of the house to the property lines.

- Transfer the measurements onto graph paper, using the graph squares as an incremental distance (for example, one square equals 1 ft., 2 ft., or more).

- Add other significant existing elements to your base plan (driveway, trees, planting beds, walls, paths, etc.), measuring from the house to the element and transferring the measurements to the graph paper.

- To relate how the inside of the house works with the outside, create a simple floor plan of the first floor within the outline of the house. Mark the location of windows and doors and any decks, porches, balconies, or terraces.

This base plan will prove invaluable throughout the rest of the design process.

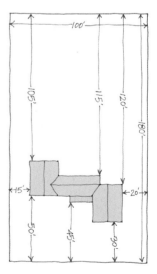

This is the kind of backyard many of us have to deal with: a wooden deck perched precariously over an exposed downhill slope with little to recommend it. (To see what the designer did with this property, turn to p. 58.)

Clearly marking the plus points and negative points on your property allows you to begin the design process from a position of strength. You know what's important to keep and what must certainly change before your property becomes the landscape you want it to be. Now let's look at the different aspects of your site in more detail.

Sun and Shade

Knowing the position of the sun in relationship to your property is critical to what you are able to do there. How your house and land are oriented—where north, south, east, and west are—affects where you choose to sit, play, plant flowers, or make a vegetable garden.

You probably have an intuitive sense of this already. You know that you like to sit in the living-room rocking chair after your morning run because you can feel the sun's rays on your back through the east-facing windows while you read the paper. In summer, you enjoy a late afternoon nap in the hammock under the oak tree that gives shade from the western sun. With trial and error, you've determined the best place for growing tomatoes on your deck—the only spot where the plants get as much as six to eight hours of sunlight, on the south side of the house. Watch the sun as it moves around your house and property, not only throughout the day but also in the different seasons. In summer, the sun is higher in the sky and days are longer. In winter, the sun sits lower in the sky and days are shorter. Knowing your property's orientation is critical to its eventual design.

The shadows cast by the house and its outbuildings and other nearby structures, or by trees and large shrubs, also play an important part in the design process. Locat-

Note the plus points (+) and negative points (-) on a sheet of tracing paper over your base plan.

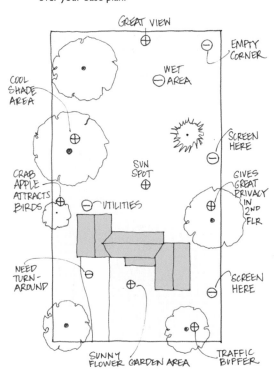

GREAT VIEW

EMPTY CORNER

COOL SHADE AREA

WET AREA

SCREEN HERE

CRAB APPLE ATTRACTS BIRDS

SUN SPOT

GIVES GREAT PRIVACY IN 2ND FLR

UTILITIES

NEED TURN-AROUND

SCREEN HERE

SUNNY FLOWER GARDEN AREA

TRAFFIC BUFFER

ing plants that require full sun versus those that can handle some degree of shade is one kind of design decision you'll need to make; another is whether you'd prefer to sit in the sun or shade at a particular time of year.

Note where the sunny spots are on your property. These are the "basking places" where you can feel the warmth of the sun's rays on your body, areas of full sun where vegetables and herbs will thrive, dogs and cats will slumber, and people will naturally gravitate to in cool weather and avoid on hot summer days.

It's equally important to establish where you can find the relief of shade on your property. Where would you choose to install a hammock to get out of the sun on a hot midsummer day? Where do you place the picnic blanket when the sun's rays beat down? These are valuable retreat spaces that need to be noted on your site plan.

Wind

Moving air caused by changes in atmospheric pressure at the earth's surface—what we more commonly know as wind—affects us in more ways than we realize. Just think back to a particularly hot and humid summer evening, and you'll appreciate that the difference between sleep and no sleep can be the presence of a night-time breeze wafting through the window. Wind lowers the ambient temperature by many degrees, making it feel cooler than it really is, and this affects the way you use your landscape. Knowing where winds come from in what season is useful information in locating terraces, decks, and other places to be on your property.

In much of the country, the benevolent winds come from the southwest in summer. Harsher storms emanate from the northeast and northwest in winter. So building a deck on the south or west side of your house allows you to enjoy summer

SUN AND SHADE

Map out the sunny areas and shady areas on your property.

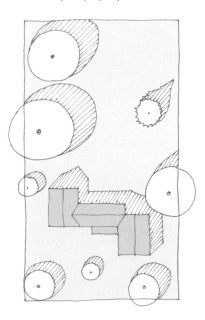

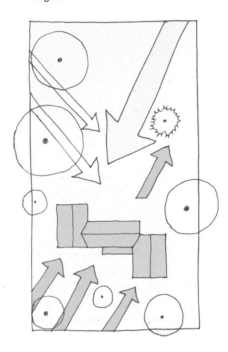

Pay attention to the prevailing winds on your site. Here, pink arrows indicate southwest summer breezes, while light blue arrows indicate northwest winter winds and dark blue arrows indicate northeast winter gales.

breezes, whereas adding a covered porch or heated breezeway on the north side can help to block prevailing winter winds.

When you combine the effects of sun, shade, and wind, you'll understand why you prefer to use different parts of your property at different times of the day and during different seasons. For instance, at my house, a deck wraps around the corner that faces south and west, enjoying cooling breezes throughout the day. With the harsh rays of the western sun beating down, my family and I normally wouldn't be able to sit there on late afternoons in summer. But, fortunately, an old oak tree provides a high canopy overhead, casting just the right amount of shade and making the deck a popular place for a late afternoon drink or an early evening barbecue.

The Ground Plane

Not all of us live on level ground but may instead face the challenges of a downhill slope or an uphill one. For instance, if your property slopes downhill, away from your house, it's hard to see and to use your landscape—and to access it easily from inside. The solution? Build terraces that create level shelves of land that step their way down the slope, with steps or staircases that connect one level to the next. One tier could be used for game playing; another as an entertainment terrace; still another might house a quiet fountain and space for just two chairs. You can maximize the use of your land when you retain each tier with stone or concrete retaining walls. Or you can use sloping hillsides to create a kind of outdoor bleacher effect—a less expensive solution but one that takes up more backyard space.

Uphill slopes can be equally challenging. On these sites, a house looks straight into a hillside, which can drain downhill into the basement if not properly graded. Such a site can loom large in relationship to the house because the land can easily

On a downhill slope, building terraces with connecting steps makes the property more accessible.

An uphill slope can present an opportunity. This house sits tight against a sloping ledge that has been turned into a front garden with the addition of creeping thyme, cotoneaster, and a few well-placed pots dripping with perennials and annuals.

overwhelm the view and make the house feel dark and dank inside. But you can overcome this obstacle by gardening the slope—making it a work of landscape art that entices rather than detracts from your view. With beautiful plantings, a winding watercourse, or stones set to draw the eye, an uphill slope can be an opportunity in disguise.

Ironically, sometimes the hardest site to deal with is one that has no slope at all. The reason? Because there are endless possibilities when you don't have any obstacles to work around. Some people choose to keep the site level and open, while others prefer to create an artificial hill or rise; some fill it up with shrubs, trees, and groves. For many, creating changes of level where there aren't any can give a back or front yard greater appeal.

GET SMART WITH SITING

You can significantly reduce heating and cooling costs simply by being smart about how you site your buildings and place trees on your property. Site your house so that it opens to the south, maximizing sun exposure in winter and southwest breezes in summer; install a large deciduous shade tree to the west to filter harsh afternoon sun; trap morning sun in the southeast to provide a basking place; and locate evergreens to the north to provide protection from severe winter winds.

Ancient cultures built according to similar principles: *feng-shui* masters suggested that a property face and drain to the south and be "backed" up by hills or vegetation behind the house to the north, east, and west, with the tallest tree or highest hill located to the northeast to ward off evil spirits that were thought to come from that direction.

ON THE LEVEL

Make slopes where none exist by redistributing soil on your property.

Existing

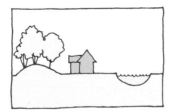

More interesting

ON A SLOPE

Use retaining walls to maximize usable space on uphill and downhill slopes.

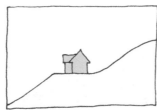

Existing

Managed slope

LEVEL GROUND

Ohio landscape designers Samuel Salsbury and Sabrena Schweyer transformed this flat backyard of grass into a vibrant outdoor living room. A wide planting bed with tall perennials covers the base of the house, and new steps link the roofed porch to a new bluestone patio that steps diagonally outward into the site. The designers also gave some focus to the backyard by building an artificial hill for a small cascade that tumbles into a pond full of fish and water plants. Nearby, a cast-iron fireplace adds warmth on cool summer evenings.

The addition of patio, pond, flower beds, and social seating area transform the once empty lawn into a three-dimensional landscape, extending the owner's living area to the outside.

(far left) Landscaping in the sandy soils of the desert requires using plants that do not need supplemental irrigation and whose natural requirements work with the local climate, a process known as *xeriscaping*.

(left) The plants that grow naturally on your land give you a clue to the type of soil you have. Here, a high shade canopy of oaks stretches over a planting of ferns, foamflowers, and heathers, all of which prefer acidic soil.

Soils

Soil composition is a complex subject that warrants a book in itself. But for the purposes of designing your landscape, there are a few things that are useful to know at the start of the design process.

Soil is the medium that supports plant growth. It's the loose layer of the earth's surface composed of rock material disintegrated by geological processes and mixed with humus (decomposed plant material). Knowing your soil type can help you decide how to improve its nutritional balance, diagnose plant problems, and apply just the right amount of fertilizers or soil amendments. Soil tests measure soil pH, the primary factor in plant growth. Most plants prefer a soil pH between 5.5 and 7.5, although there are some acid-loving exceptions such as rhododendrons, blueberries, and potatoes.

You can often determine the type of soil you have by noting which plants grow naturally on your land. For example, if you have a naturally occurring grove of oak and hemlock trees nearby, you probably have acid soil and can grow companion plants like rhododendrons and mountain laurel. Maple, elm, and ash trees prefer sweeter soil. Some plants like "wet feet"—their roots in damp soil; others require drier conditions. Noting which plants thrive naturally on your property is one way to figure out what other plants you can grow there.

Vegetation

Unless you've bought a house that sits on a completely cleared site, your property is made up of existing vegetation—trees, shrubs, and ground covers—that you need to evaluate as you think about what to create there. Plantings are to the home outside what carpets, window coverings, and upholstery are to the inside of your house—

DID YOU KNOW?

You can test your soil by sending a sample to your county agricultural extension service. Sample six or more separate locations around your house and mix them together to make a composite. You'll receive a report about the quality of your soil, the kinds of vegetation it can support, and any amendments that should be added to it.

To locate existing trees on your base plan (see p. 23), take measurements from the trunk to the corners of your house (or property lines).

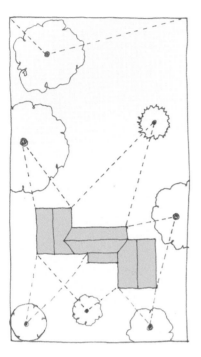

The blue-green feathery foliage of the Powis Castle Sage highlights the bright red berries of the American Cranberry Bush in fall. These two plants would surely be keepers in any existing garden.

they soften the structure of spaces and bestow different personalities by their varying shapes, textures, and colors. Look around you, making note of what appeals to you and what doesn't. Notice whether you have any special trees—ones that are larger than others around them, or have a more interesting form, flowering habit, or leaf color in the fall. These trees are keepers, of course, and may take on focal importance as you design. Groupings of trees, such as an orchard, a grove, or a woodland or forest, add magic to a landscape, since they offer an overhead canopy for getting out from under the sun and a shady microclimate for growing a different palette of plants.

You're also likely to have shrubs and ground covers on your property. Often these take the form of overgrown foundation plantings that require hacking back every year before they get so high that they block out views from inside. Consider removing—or moving—them to give your house some breathing room. After all, of the many items that you spend money on to fix up your house, plants may offer the best value. Planted in the right place and cared for properly, most vegetation will

(far left) Two large shade trees encircled by cobblestones frame this newly planted landscape, while buff-colored gravel paths provide access from the driveway along the picket fence to the paved front walk.

(left) Purple heathers sweep down a hillside filled with silver, green, and variegated foliage.

grow quickly after just a small investment in time and materials. Record the location of the plants on your property, noting what you hope to save, move to a different location, or remove completely.

It's not easy for most laypeople to identify the plants they have on their property. At the very least, you can note whether a plant is evergreen—it keeps its leaves or needles throughout the year—or deciduous—it loses its leaves or needles during the winter. You can note the shape of the plant: whether it's upright, vase-shaped, rounded, prostrate (running along the ground), spiky, or weeping. It helps to jot down the attributes of your plants throughout the year: when they leaf out, flower, and lose their leaves, for instance. Your local county extension service can also be helpful if you want to identify your plants—taking in a stalk or branch will allow horticulturists to figure out the particular plant species.

Circulation

The land around your house is the first thing you see when you set foot on your property and the last thing you experience as you leave. Therefore, how you move from outside to inside and back again is an important part of understanding your existing site. We will discuss circulation and flow in detail in the chapter "Making It Flow" on p. 140, but for now as you evaluate your site, note the different routes you take as you drive into, enter, or walk around your property. Do they work well as they are or need changing? Make an overlay sketch of how circulation in and around your house and land works right now. This may change as you move through the design process.

How a person moves from point A (the driveway, for instance) to point B (the front door) may not always be well enough marked or established for you or your guests. I've seen houses with an elaborate front walkway that leads from sidewalk to front door but that has no path that connects the driveway to the front entry. I've also experienced pathways that lead nowhere and benches that can't be reached. As we'll see in "Making It Flow," the way you move from landscape into house and back out again directly affects your experience of the whole.

MAPPING THE FLOW

Make a sketch of how you currently move into, out of, and around your house and property.

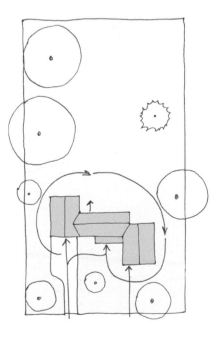

Identify the most important views
that you want to preserve.

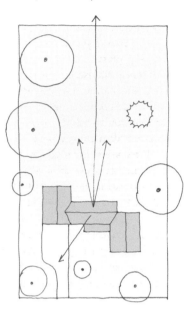

If you're fortunate enough to enjoy a spectacular view, make sure to note it on your
site analysis plan.

Views and Special Features

An important part of every site is the views it affords, both good and bad. Some homeowners may be lucky enough to enjoy long views out to an attractive land-scape feature, such as a river, a mountain, or a canyon. For others, the view may be a problem—a nearby apartment building, the neighbor's derelict chain-link fence, or your own unsightly garage. Concealing or revealing these views is an important part of improving your home outside. As you evaluate your site, jot down those views that you want to play up and those that you hope to block on your analysis plan.

Also note the special features that set your property apart. Perhaps your house enjoys a great view of the rising or setting sun or has a handsome outcrop of ledge at the back of the yard. Make sure to ask each member of your family what his or her favorite part of the yard is. You may be surprised at their answers. The husband of a friend of mine failed to indicate the importance of a bamboo grove where his kids loved to play and had a landscaper clear away every existing tree and shrub on his

Take away the landscaping around this Arts and Crafts bungalow and it loses much of its curb appeal. Matching the picket fence to the red trim relates the fence to the architecture of the house and plays up the value of the garden in between the two.

property, replacing them with a bland expanse of lawn. Imagine his chagrin when he realized that he had, without asking, removed a favorite outdoor play space.

Budget Considerations

Everyone has a budget that helps define the scope and extent of any project. As with building or renovating a house, developing a landscape takes more resources than we may be prepared to spend. On top of this, most of us overspend on our house, leaving little money left over for making improvements to our property (which is a good reason to include a budget for landscaping from the very start for any large-scale home-improvement project you undertake).

Just how much should a landscape budget be? While there's no magic formula, my rule of thumb is that renovating a landscape can cost as much as remodeling a kitchen—a worthwhile investment given that they are both critical to your sense of comfort and pleasure. A beautiful landscape also improves property values. Realtors acknowledge that a house with "curb appeal" in the front and a well-designed private landscape in the back can add as much as 20 percent to the value of your home.

Yet few of us enjoy unlimited resources. Rather than paying for an entire reworking of the landscape, you can phase your expenditures over several years, as explained in the chapter "Big Moves" on p. 50. With careful planning, guided by a landscape professional, you can create a master plan that suggests the order in which the different projects should be addressed.

Another way to stay within budget is to landscape your home yourself. Certainly, digging out planting beds, installing ground covers, shrubs, and even trees, laying sod, and spreading mulch are all projects that do not necessarily have to be done by a professional landscaping contractor.

WORKING WITH PROFESSIONALS

One of my goals in writing this book is to help you understand my design process so that you can create your ideal landscape yourself or with the help of professionals in the field. If you choose the latter course, this book will guide you as you move through the process with them, enabling you to ask the right questions and demand the best answers.

There are many kinds of landscape professionals, each with his or her own way of working. **Landscape architects,** registered by the state they live in, typically have a master's degree in landscape architecture, have worked for fellow professionals for three or more years, and have undergone an arduous test to get certified. As a result, they are often highly skilled in the technical aspects of a project, such as grading and drainage design. While many landscape architects specialize in residential projects, others do not, working instead on public large-scale parks and streetscapes.

Landscape designers and **landscape gardeners** tend to have less technical training, specializing in horticulture, botany, or landscape design. **Landscape contractors,** also known as landscapers, are good at building projects but are not necessarily trained in how to design them.

I hope you will read through this whole book, taking notes, doing the exercises, drawing plans, and even dog-earing the pages to keep track of the ideas that resonate with you. Whether or not you hire a professional, the same process applies, with the same desired outcome: creating a home outside that gets you and your family out onto your land in the most enjoyable way possible.

SLIPPERY SLOPE: TURNING A PROBLEM INTO AN OPPORTUNITY

When Kirsten Siebert, one of the principals of Broadleaf Landscape Architecture, first arrived at this small piece of land located just across a dirt road from the Mad River in northern Vermont, she saw a charming historic home and barn that sat below an overgrown hillside. Remnants of old stone walls and gardens dotted the property. Except for an existing front porch, there was no place to sit and enjoy the sounds and sights of the nearby river.

Kirsten decided to connect the two buildings by means of new stone terraces and walls. She chose a circular form that maximized the seating area, designing a built-in grill, handsome semicircular steps, and native plantings. During construction, the overgrown plantings on the upward slope were removed to reveal a massive ledge.

Kirsten saw the ledge as an opportunity in disguise. Wanting to provide access to all parts of the upward-sloping backyard, she worked with a local mason to turn the ledge

The front porch, before and after landscaping.

into an asset, carving a narrow set of steps out of stone. The steps lead to a pair of log chairs on a stone terrace at the very top of their land. Above the hewn steps, Kirsten planted blueberry bushes and an orchard set into a wildflower meadow that attracts birds and butterflies to the property. A level croquet lawn that sits above the house leads to a small village park nearby. What others might have seen as a problem—the stony wall of ledge—became the most special feature of all, thanks to Kirsten's ingenuity and a stonemason's skill.

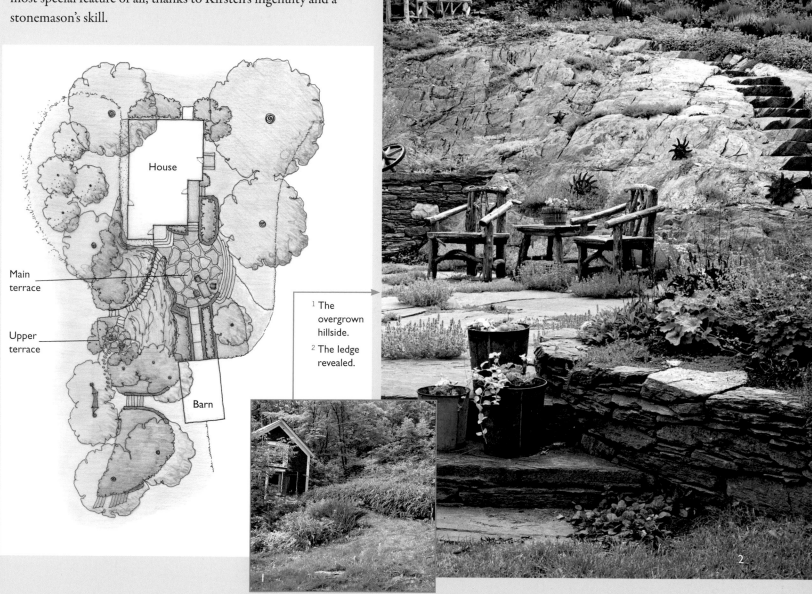

House

Main terrace

Upper terrace

Barn

1 The overgrown hillside.
2 The ledge revealed.

1 The wildflower meadow looking down toward the barn.

2 A local stonemason carved a narrow set of steps into the ledge, providing access to the terrace at the top of the slope.

3 A new stone terrace connects the house and barn, with an outdoor fireplace for roasting hot dogs and marshmallows on summer nights.

4 The stone terrace at the top of the property looks down over the ledge.

(above left and right) Don't be afraid to dream big while you imagine your ideal site. Although most of us don't have a natural pond on our property, it can provide the inspiration to make a smaller version in your own backyard.

(below) Your pets make their home outside as much as you do and should have a "voice" in how it is designed. Make a note of their favorite sun spots and shady retreats.

Your Ideal Site

Once you've completed the analysis of your actual site, you know a great deal about your property, its qualities, and the elements that make it special. Now you're ready to move on to figuring out what your ideal site might look like. Whether you recognize it or not, you already know a lot about what you want your property to become: You've unconsciously been collecting ideas for your own landscape from earliest childhood until the present day. Now it's time to use these ideas to help you identify the components of your ideal site.

A big part of imagining your ideal site is understanding your own character, your interests, your preferences, and your dreams—the very things that will make your particular site unique. Don't overlook the preferences of your spouse, your children, and other loved ones who live with you (even your cats and dogs!). Discovering your individual and collective "designer's personality" helps explain what you need to maintain and to change about your existing property to bring it into line with your ideal (see the test on pp. 40–41).

To know the elements of your ideal site, you'll need to look at a range of issues, including the special places that have influenced you in the past, the activity options you are drawn to, your aesthetic preferences, and your preferred "places to be."

(facing page) A hammock in a shady corner: Who doesn't long for a setting like this in his or her own backyard? All you need are two trees just the right distance apart.

WHAT KIND OF DESIGNER ARE YOU?

Figure out what kind of aesthetic style you have by taking the following test. Choose between each of the following pairs, circling the answer that best describes you. Each part has five questions; add up your score for each part separately.

Part I

1. **Do you prefer to be:**
   a. Outside in your landscape by yourself?
   b. Outside in the company of others?

2. **Is your landscape a place:**
   a. That you prefer to work in or walk through by yourself?
   b. That you prefer to share with family, friends, and neighbors?

3. **Do you prefer that your property:**
   a. Feel private and hidden from the public?
   b. Be open to view by neighbors and passersby?

4. **Would you rather have a terrace:**
   a. That's just big enough for an intimate twosome?
   b. That's large enough for entertaining and social gatherings?

5. **Would you prefer to:**
   a. Begin the design of your garden on your own?
   b. Talk over your garden design with others?

Part II

6. **Are you concerned with:**
   a. Making the details of your landscape work?
   b. Envisioning the overall aesthetic of your landscape?

7. **Do you prefer choices that are:**
   a. Tried and true?
   b. New, different, and cutting edge?

8. **Do you like to:**
   a. Make small changes to your existing landscape?
   b. Transform your surroundings into something completely different?

9. **If money were no object:**
   a. Would you prefer to plant and maintain your landscape by yourself?
   b. Would you hire help to do the work for you?

10. **Do you prefer to stay informed about:**
    a. New plant introductions?
    b. Or design trends?

Part III

11. **Do you make decisions about your landscape:**
    a. Based on established design principles?
    b. Based on what you would instinctively like it to be?

12. **When you landscape your property, do you feel more comfortable:**
    a. Following expert advice?
    b. Following your own feelings about how it should look?

13. **Do you tend to prefer:**
    a. Placing objects in logical rows or geometric patterns?
    b. Arranging objects in a whimsical pattern of your own choosing and design?

14. **Do you tend to focus:**
    a. On a single "right" idea?
    b. Or do you see many ways that might work just as well?

15. **Do you look at your landscape:**
    a. In a highly critical way?
    b. Or are you more accepting of how it looks right now?

Part IV

16. **Do you design:**
    a. On paper and then plant exactly according to plan?
    b. On a whim?

Reserved

Expressive

Practical

Conceptual

17. *Do you prepare your beds:*

    a. Before shopping for plants?

    b. As you install them?

18. *Do you like your property:*

    a. To be neat and well kept?

    b. To be a little bit wild and unkempt?

19. *Do you tend to:*

    a. Work on and finish up one project at a time?

    b. Have several projects going at once?

20. *Do you like to:*

    a. Stick with the plans at hand?

    b. Make changes to your plans as you go?

Scoring: Add a separate score for each part of the test. Give 1 point for all (a) responses; 2 points for all (b) responses. If you scored . . .

Part I: (5–7) You're a Reserved Designer

You prefer creating a landscape that offers calm, quiet solitude where you can meet friends on a one-on-one basis. You are a reserved person who tends to like contained spaces to get away from the workaday world. Your private landscape expresses your inner world and experiences.

(8–10) You're an Expressive Designer

You prefer to create a landscape that is for socializing in small and large groups. It reflects your gregarious and cheerful disposition. You like expressing your enthusiasms and interests on your property, and you love introducing others to what you've created.

Part II: (5–7) You're a Practical Designer

You're a realist who likes concrete facts, literal ideas, sensible information, and tried-and-true choices. You understand the world through your senses and are interested in creating a landscape that is a practical place with utility value.

(8–10) You're a Conceptual Designer

You're an abstract thinker who loves the imaginative, conceptual world of patterns and theories. You are a bit unconventional and love anything inventive and new. Your landscape planning focuses on the concept and not its application. You work toward the future and are open to change.

Part III: (5–7) You're a Principled Designer

You're a person who prefers logical analysis and precise, tough-minded critiques. You live by precepts and principles and prefer a landscape that is based on scientific or theoretical ideals rather than personal values. You like clarity of form and structure and often have an environmental ethic that informs your landscaping decisions.

(8–10) You're a Personal Designer

You landscape by feeling, rather than through a set of preconceived principles. You want to create a harmonious place that is enjoyable for yourself as well as others. You prefer to include everyone's ideas and feelings in your designs. You like your property to express your personal ideals and to show off your likes and dislikes.

Part IV: (5–7) You're an Orderly Designer

You prefer an organized, structured life that includes careful planning for all events. Your property is carefully organized and maintained. You do your landscape planning on paper ahead of time and are careful to follow plans.

(8–10) You're a Relaxed Designer

You prefer a casual approach to landscaping, where decisions are made spontaneously, and you feel no compunction about plunging in without detailed plans. Your landscape follows no particular structure, and you love to design as you go. You like a leisurely pace and enjoy being surprised each year by the property's progress.

Principled

Personal

Orderly

Relaxed

(above) Whenever the author travels, she visits natural landscapes and gardens to add to her "collection" of beautiful places that inspire ideas and images for her work. This garden is in Ravello, Italy.

(below right) Here we go round, the mulberry bush . . ." As children, many of us loved places where we could look out but feel we couldn't be seen.

Special Places

You and your loved ones carry within you images of special places that have affected you from earliest childhood. Take a moment to remember them. Think back to your childhood daydreaming places—natural or built spaces where you went to play on your own or with a close friend. Write them down, draw them, or find images on the Internet or in magazines that represent them, noting how you felt at the time. Move forward in time to the present day, remembering special trips, holidays, garden spots, public parks, or natural landscapes that are meaningful to you. Each offers food for inspiration throughout the design process. Revisit and add to the list as you read on, and you'll be able to work some of these ideas into your plans for the home outside.

To understand someone's ideal landscape, my favorite question to ask is: Where did you go as a child for daydreaming, reverie, and reflection? I've had clients who mention a grandmother's garden or a hiding place beneath a rhododendron bush. Others talk about places by the sea or high in the mountains. Interior spaces such as bedrooms or libraries are also popular choices. These early memories of pleasurable spaces are reminders of what's possible for your own landscape.

Here's an example of how the special places you have known may inspire the design of your landscape. A client of mine is of Portuguese ancestry. In his tiny back-yard courtyard in a northeastern city, he wanted to bring some of his heritage into

(above left) For someone who loves to bake, having an outside pizza oven is a dream come true.

(above right) An old-fashioned house encourages old-fashioned activities, with rocking chairs on a porch and a swing hanging from an old maple tree to remind us to kick back and relax.

the designs for his garden. We ended up creating wrought-iron sculptures as focal points that were based on the maritime influences of his past. Another client remembered visiting her grandmother's formal rose garden as a child, a place she loved more than any other. For her small urban backyard, we created a tiny version of her beloved childhood memory place.

Activity Options

Think about how you want to use your property. Write down a list of all the activities you and your family would like to see happen there. Depending on its size, your property may not be able to fit too many of these options, but it doesn't hurt to dream at this stage (and it costs nothing!).

The possibilities, of course, are endless: creating family play spaces for lawn sports and ball play; building a swimming or dipping pool, pond, or hot tub; making a space for outdoor grilling, barbecuing, or smoking; locating places for celebrating, entertaining, dining al fresco, or quiet contemplation; finding special spots for birdwatching, sunbathing, or stargazing; making a vegetable or herb garden or an orchard; creating beautiful perennial borders, a rose garden, or a wildflower meadow.

Aesthetic Preferences

As you think about your ideal site, it's inevitable that you and your loved ones will have different aesthetic preferences from one other. For instance, your spouse may prefer a landscape that is formal, organized, and spare, while your son likes spaces that are informal, casual, and filled up. The photos below, which show a wide range of contrasting aesthetic qualities, will help you identify these various preferences. Have each member of your family indicate the ones that are most appealing. This information will be invaluable as you move through the rest of the design process.

Don't be surprised if you and your spouse respond differently to the pairings. For example, you may love a more traditional look to your landscape, with a symmetrical layout, straight lines, and vertical elements built for large-group dining. Your spouse may prefer the opposite: a low-slung, informal landscape of curves and bright colors that's basically contemplative in nature. How do you reconcile the two? One

AESTHETIC PAIRINGS

Formal Informal

Symmetrical Asymmetrical

Contemplative Social

Horizontal Vertical

Flat Rolling

way is to make sure to locate both kinds of spaces—gathering and getaway, each with the opposite aesthetic—on different parts of your property, as we'll see in the chapter "Comfort Zones" on p. 84. But on a very small site, you'll have to make some accommodations: Maybe the deck right off the house has a formal look with a pergola and vertical columns, while a circular patio below the level of the deck sits in the sunny spot, surrounded by bright-colored containers of flowers.

Places to Be

Where are the places you most love to be—both inside and outside the house? I believe there are seven distinct vantage points we're drawn to in natural settings, built landscapes, or architecture. I call these the "seven archetypes": the sea, the cave, the harbor, the promontory, the island, the mountain, and the sky. Each archetype has a distinct form that matches the feeling you experience when you inhabit it.

Representational Abstract

Spare Filled up

Dark light

Straight Curved

Intimate Immense

KEEPING A SCRAPBOOK

Make a scrapbook of the ideas, images, and qualities that you'd like to reproduce on your property. Find photographs from books or magazines, images from the Internet, color chips, samples of plant material—all the things that you'd love to incorporate into your design. Keep gathering clippings as you work through the book. You'll return again and again to your scrapbook as you gather ideas, turning them into real-life spaces when you finally begin building your dream landscape.

Keeping a scrapbook of images and ideas is a useful tool in planning your home outside. As you look at these selections, you can imagine what this landscape will look like—full of red, orange, and violet flowers with a splash of blue for contrast.

Look through the following list and note the vantage points that most appeal to you. Which do you have on your property? Which do you wish you had?

The Sea: You delight in feeling surrounded or immersed.

The Cave: You enjoy occupying a form-fitting space.

The Harbor: You like to feel enclosed, as in embracing arms.

The Promontory: You like to perch out over the edge.

The Island: You like being in the middle of an open space.

The Mountain: You prefer being on top of a high place.

The Sky: You imagine leaving the landscape behind.

When you are aware of your own spatial preferences, you can more easily create such vantage points in your own backyard. If you love high places, you might want to build a tower, a tree house, or a mound—and put a bench there. If you prefer enclosed spaces, you might construct a writing hut, a summerhouse, or a gazebo. If you want a view of the sky, you can simply place a chaise lounge in an open spot on your lawn. And nothing says that you can't create all seven vantage points somewhere on your property. We'll return to these ideas in later chapters. Keep them in mind as you work your way through the rest of the design process.

Sea

Cave

Harbor

Promontory

Island

Mountain

Sky

REFLECTING THE SKY

Overlooking the San Gabriel Mountains near Los Angeles, this house and landscape are a good example of how one designer turned a host of site problems into a dramatic but simple home outside. When landscape designer Mia Lehrer of ML+A first visited the property (the "actual site"), the view from the narrow sliver of land was completely blocked by overgrown shrubs and the backyard was dominated by a two-car garage and vast expanse of concrete. Traffic noise from a local freeway was also a problem. The owner asked for a privacy wall, a lap pool, and a cutting garden, with a palette of drought-resistant plants that would thrive in the dry climate (her "ideal site").

Mia found inspiration for her landscape design in the owner's collection of modernist furniture, developing a spare and elegant design that couples the colors of southern California skies with the stark landscape materials that match the house. A long blue concrete wall encloses the property and gives harborlike privacy to part of the swimming pool. Cast-in-place concrete terraces anchor both ends of the pool, providing delightful sun spots for gathering. Turning the site drawbacks into opportunities, Mia has created a surprisingly expansive landscape on a long, narrow site.

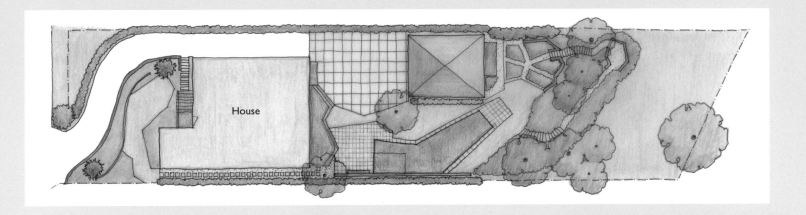

¹ The existing site.

² A 40-ft.-long lap pool with spa follows the property line, backed up by a mottled blue wall whose color connects the water of the pool to the dramatic blue sky.

³ Following the sight lines, the angled lap pool opens up to the view, creating a promontory-like edge condition that echoes the land formation beyond.

⁴ Stainless-steel pegs in the wall form water droplets when it rains, diffusing the traffic sounds and bringing movement to the surface of the pool.

Big Moves

At the heart of any good design is one or more "big moves"—a set of organizing strategies that pulls the different parts of a landscape together. In this chapter, I explain what form these strategies can take and how to use them to make effective design decisions for your landscape. It's amazing but true: When you know what big moves you'd like to make on your property, then all the details begin to fall right into place.

Regardless of the size or shape of your property, there are three types of big moves that can help organize its design. First, you select a basic layout; second, choose an aesthetic arrangement; and third, identify a distinctive theme. Let's look at each.

"An idea is salvation by imagination."

—FRANK LLOYD WRIGHT

Select a Basic Layout

Different layouts or arrangements address the way you'd like to live on your land. I've narrowed these down to four fundamental ways of organizing your landscape: Immersed or Exposed, Central Clearing, House Front and Center, and Open-Air Rooms. Depending on the orientation, vegetation, size, and shape of your land, you may find that one layout suits your situation better than the others (although you can also combine two or more layouts). Let's take a typical site and sketch out each basic layout (see the drawing on the facing page). When you've read through them all, select the one that best suits you and your property. See the drawings on the facing page.

Immersed or Exposed

Many of us start out with a property that hasn't been developed as a home outside. We might live in an old house on an uncleared site (immersed) or in a new house on

Some Immersed layouts are inherently appealing, as is the case with this wildflower meadow that extends all the way to the house.

a cleared lot (exposed). These seemingly opposite conditions have similarly contrasting problems and opportunities. Neither starts with an existing layout, but each offers chances to improve the particular site and situation.

In an immersed setting, a house can feel delightfully dwarfed by its surroundings, like a campsite in the wilderness or a cabin set deep in the woods. With little direct exposure to the sun, it's difficult to grow or nurture many plants that might live under the overstory. Instead, a subtle but handsome display of native ground covers and mosses may predominate underfoot. But sometimes you can create the immersed condition in an exposed setting by filling up the spaces around your house with plants. Inveterate gardeners do this all the time.

In an exposed setting, a house sits alone on bare land—typically former farmland that's been developed or woodland that's been clear-cut. Sometimes the exposed condition may be just what you want: If you live in a desert, on a ranch, or on abutting pasture land, for example, you are probably drawn to wide-open spaces. Leaving

(far left) **People who love plants enjoy the Immersed experience. Here, sliding doors open onto a tiny triangular deck sized just for two and surrounded by a sea of foliage.**

(left) **Sometimes an Exposed setting needs little in the way of landscaping. This open pasture was artfully turned into an asset by designing a handsome angular retaining wall and placing a large shade tree at the corner of the clean lines of the house.**

BASIC LAYOUTS

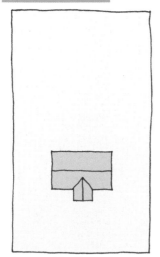

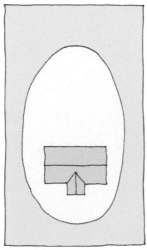

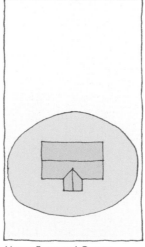

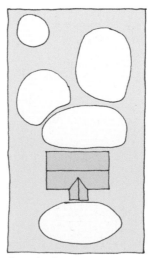

Immersed (or Exposed)   Central Clearing   House Front and Center   Open-Air Rooms

your landscape simple and open, except for planting the occasional tree for the relief of shade, may satisfy your needs. But for the rest of us who are coping with unwanted exposure, this condition is ripe for a big move: Any of the next three layouts would improve this type of site.

Central Clearing

Early homesteaders felled trees to form openings in a forest, clearings that let in light and air for growing their gardens and grazing their livestock. Similarly, you can choose a layout where you make a clearing around your home by planting the perimeter and leaving it open at the center. In this scenario, you create usable open space— for play, games, sunbathing, or entertaining—directly outside the house, with a privacy screen or barrier surrounding the whole. Unlike the immersed layout, you and your house enjoy breathing room that brings sunlight and fresh air into indoor and outdoor living spaces. Another benefit is that views between house and landscape

A Central Clearing layout doesn't have to be grand or high maintenance. The rectangular brick terrace above nestles next to the house, adorned only by chaise longues and containers of tomatoes and herbs, while the simple circle of slate at right is surrounded by plantings and backed up by a wall of climbing hydrangea.

and between landscape and house can be designed in tandem, bringing harmony to the whole property.

Problems with the Central Clearing layout occur when the house sits high off the ground or has an elevated foundation that remains exposed unless plantings are introduced to hide it. When this happens, you can extend the perimeter screen to include the house, veiling it with hedging or garden beds, while keeping the middle open for use. This "hole in the donut" effect can be any shape you want and filled with any number of possibilities: a lawn panel, meadow grasses, a swimming pool or pond, or terracing, to name a few. The Central Clearing can be as big or small as your property can accommodate.

House Front and Center

The house at the front of the lot parallel to the street is the most typical layout of homes in the United States, and it makes the house the most dominant landscape feature on a property. Foundation plantings surround the building, which serves as a backdrop for trees, shrubs, and ground covers. Adjacent trees can filter light and bring shade to interiors with too much sun. When it's done well, deep beds and generous plantings seem to "settle" the house into its land.

There are problems to consider with this kind of layout. Because foundation plantings ornament and set off the house, it's often hard to find "places to be" in this type of landscape. When plantings are used only as layers against the house, they aren't carving out outdoor living spaces. Instead, areas for sitting and playing are assigned to the leftover areas between planting beds and property line—a kind of visual no-man's land. Another problem with the House Front and Center layout is that the foundation plantings, especially if they are overgrown shrubs, don't allow for enough light and air around the house. Besides covering up windows and scratching paint, leggy, unkempt plantings can also cause mold and mildew problems in the basement.

(above left) The House Front and Center layout, with the house parallel to the street, is the most common layout for homes in the United States.

(above right) This generous planting bed filled with black-eyed Susans curves out to meet a bluestone path set into the lawn. The plants are cut back away from the wall of the house to allow in light and air around the foundation.

DRIP EDGE

If you choose to install foundation plantings around the base of your house, make sure to leave a yard or more of gravel around the drip line (even if you have gutters).

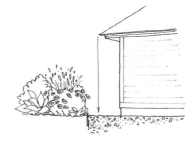

VICTORIAN MAKEOVER

A house always looks better when framed by elegant foundation plantings rather than a bare, tired suburban lawn. This stately Victorian sat exposed on a corner lot in full "front and center" position before Chux Landscaping arrived on the scene. They removed the existing horseshoe-shaped driveway and installed a simple, straight walkway at the side of the lot to open up the site to plantings and a lawn. Using period plantings such as hollies, hostas, ferns, and astilbes, the landscapers created layered perennials on either side of a border of holly along the street edge to provide a degree of privacy from passersby. They also moved a mature holly tree closer to the house to act as a screen for a small sitting terrace and installed broad beds of plantings along the foundation.

Newly installed beds of naturalistic plantings along the foundation elegantly set off the house and provide a garden that blooms throughout the year.

Open-Air Rooms

As more and more people discover the joys of outdoor living, they are choosing to create Open-Air Rooms around their property. This is a simple way to lay out your property: All you need to do is to make outdoor sitting spaces in the places you want to be. You can construct one or more terraces, a deck, a platform, or a series of garden enclosures that hold a swimming pool, an herb garden, or even a secret garden behind lock and key.

Like the Central Clearing layout, this approach opens up areas to light and air while using enclosures or plant material as a border around the perimeter. The difference is that each separate "room" has the potential to be developed individually. Without a thoughtful master plan, creating a series of Open-Air Rooms over time can result in a hodgepodge of spaces that don't hold together visually or aesthetically. But if you have a clear sense of the layout you're seeking to achieve, you can develop your property in phases or all at once, depending upon your budget.

(below left) Two Open-Air Rooms—one for children, one for adults—coexist harmoniously in this backyard, with the same curving form used to define both spaces.

(below right) An Open-Air Room doesn't have to be large or elaborate to be effective. This tiny pea-stone terrace edged with cobblestones provides a contemplative corner for two.

LANDSCAPING IN PHASES

No matter how big or small the property we own, most of us live on a budget and can't afford to develop our home outside without phasing the work over time. The owners of this Vermont property didn't know much about landscaping before they hired Paul Wieczoreck of Champlain Valley Landscaping and Kirsten Seibert of Broadleaf Landscape Architecture to help them place foundation plantings around the high deck at the front of the house. Little did they know that, by the time they finished some 10 years later, they would

have built a number of Open-Air Rooms and, in the process, turned into accomplished gardeners themselves.

Broadleaf came up with a "conceptual master plan" for the property before launching into any major changes. A master plan develops concepts for spatial relationships around the house, including early ideas for the location of hardscaping, planting areas, and major trees. It also lays out a phasing schedule, so that different parts of the site can be developed over time—useful even for those clients with the deepest of pockets.

Ten years ago, the house and landscape looked very different than they do today. An old wooden deck was removed to make way for beautiful plantings. Stone retaining walls hold up a terrace with wrought-iron railings. Ornamental trees, shrubs, and ground covers cascade down the hillside, making a handsome base of support for the house.

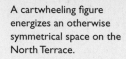

Because it really deals with the flow between spaces, a good master plan needs to be flexible over a long period of time.

As the designers returned each year to work on a new space, the previously landscaped spaces influenced what they created there next. In the words of one of the principals, "One of the benefits of taking a slower pace when you phase your landscape is that you change your ideas once the site begins to take shape."

The designers began with the Entry Garden, which acts as an outdoor foyer by the kitchen door. Next up was the North Terrace,

A cartwheeling figure energizes an otherwise symmetrical space on the North Terrace.

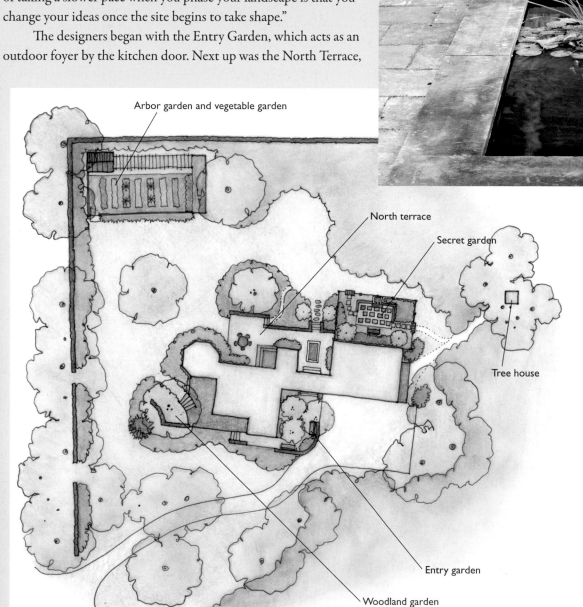

Arbor garden and vegetable garden

North terrace

Secret garden

Tree house

Entry garden

Woodland garden

where they created a brick and bluestone patio centered on a small oblong pool with a joyous cartwheeling figure as focal point. The Arbor Garden was built the third year—constructed of logs that blew down in a storm—followed by the Vegetable Garden, set in a sunny back corner of the property.

The magnum opus is the Secret Garden that sits directly behind the garage. This contemplative garden looks out through an octagonal window in the handsome wooden fence to a labyrinth created by the owner in the adjacent woods. A potting shed was next—a necessary addition as the owner became more and more involved in maintaining her garden. After the Woodland Garden was installed, the pair began work on the Tree House , a little hut set up on stilts on part of their property that they are just beginning to develop. This writer's retreat looks into the foliage of the native oak, birch, and maple trees around it and is filled with the owner's beloved items (including her dog).

1 A vegetable garden sits in the sunniest corner of the site, backed up by a pergola and sitting hut made of cedar trees that were downed in a storm.

2 Glimpsed through an octagonal window cut into the wooden fence, the Secret Garden sits behind the garage, a contemplative sitting area centered on a focal pond and a Chinese red bench.

3 The latest phase of the 10-year design process is a tree house that sits on stilts in a wooded section of the site. Built of rough-hewn logs, the tree house's wooden floor holds up a porch swing and a hammock underneath.

4 The tree house is the ultimate getaway space, also serving as an indoor/outdoor study, sleeping porch, and doggy haven.

This Open-Air Room sits within a larger Central Clearing with an Immersed forest beyond. The wrought-iron seating sits on its own "terrace" of grass enclosed by a "wall" of multihued perennials.

Mix and Match

Each of the four layouts can be mixed and matched, depending upon the size and configuration of your property. For instance, the Vermont couple whose house is featured on p. 58 chose to leave more than half of their four acres forested, not only for ease of maintenance but also because they liked being able to walk in their own woods. On a much smaller half-acre suburban property, you could also leave the back half in woodland for the same reasons. Keeping a stand of trees, bamboo, or meadow grasses—Immersed or Exposed—somewhere on your lot brings you a different kind of pleasure than opening up the whole site to the elements.

As we've seen, you can also use plantings up against the house, making it Front and Center along one face, and open up the other to create a Central Clearing there instead. And, like the Vermont couple, you can create Open-Air Rooms both adjacent to and far away from the house.

Each of these three small landscapes demonstrates a different aesthetic arrangement.

(right) All Lined Up shows a landscape whose plantings feel informal in spite of the symmetrical layout.

(facing page left) On the Angle features staggered wooden platforms that act like bridges through a river of verdant plantings.

(facing page right) Voluptuous Curves highlights a curvilinear brick terrace softened by a high canopy of trees. Each arrangement sets a distinct mood in these otherwise similar spaces.

Choose an Aesthetic Arrangement

Once you've selected your basic layout or a hybrid of several types, you can choose to arrange it in one of three ways, which I call All Lined Up, On the Angle, or Voluptuous Curves. This is a good time to look back at the "Aesthetic Preferences" list on pp. 44–45. Remind yourself: Are you drawn to symmetry or asymmetry? Do you prefer formal or informal? Traditional or contemporary? Straight or curved? Knowing these preferences helps you decide how to overlay the layout you've selected with an aesthetic arrangement that fits you and your family. As with the four basic layouts, these arrangements can also be mixed and matched at will. Let's start with the basics.

(facing page) Symmetry is an inherently satisfying arrangement, but once you start it's hard to stop. Here, matching clipped evergreens step down a far wall to frame a sculptural fire pit. Handsome pots flank a garden pool.

(far left) It's satisfying to choose an arrangement that lines up with the elements of your house or outbuildings. By doing so, you meld architecture with landscape so that the two begin to intertwine into one designed whole.

(left) Using the geometry of the house to locate landscape elements extends the presence of home onto your property. Here, a high deck just off the kitchen serves as the reference point for a brick walkway topped by a wooden pergola that leads from the driveway to the backyard.

All Lined Up

If you like clear organization, formality, or symmetry, this is the ideal aesthetic for you. When you line up what's outside so that it relates to what's inside, you give your landscape a definite structure that can be developed over time. Furthermore, when landscape elements are aligned with an element of your house, such as a door, a window, or a gable end, you establish a sense of harmony between them.

Elements that are misaligned can seem unsettled and visually jarring. Anything even slightly askew can feel wrong—a crooked statue, a fence or wall that's not quite level, or an apple orchard with one tree out of line. Objects don't need to relate symmetrically to be satisfying, but some type of alignment brings a comforting sense of order to a landscape. Why is alignment important to us? It might be that we possess an innate need to exercise control over our environments, arranging them to echo our own biaxial bodies.

Use your house for reference points Your house—typically the biggest three-dimensional object on your property—acts as a powerful reference point for other landscape elements, organizing what might otherwise feel random and unsettling. Therefore, when you align elements in a landscape with those of the house, you establish an invisible reference line that relates the two and brings a sense of order.

The more formal the style of a house and garden, the more it pays to be finicky about alignments. Deviations from the chosen pattern will tend to stand out. Orienting exterior structures and landscape features to the architecture of your home can offer you many options for interconnecting house and land. When you pay attention to alignment, you will help bring your whole property into harmony.

ALL LINED UP

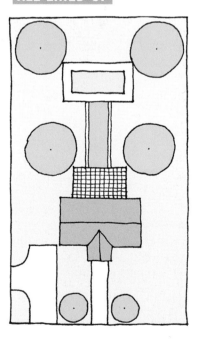

LINE IT UP

A great starting point for a landscape's design is to identify the visual lines that relate to the exterior doors, windows, and corners of your house and other buildings on your property. Then place outside elements so that they are on axis with these lines.

- A path can be located on an axis with a front or back door or between porch columns.

- A fence or shrub border looks pleasing if it runs parallel or perpendicular to a house.

- A terrace can be aligned within the space between a house and a garage.

- The rhythm of window placement on the face of your house can suggest a way to space rosebushes or fence posts along the front of your lot.

Although this landscape is not symmetrical, it nevertheless feels completely balanced. Perhaps it's because the central path bisects the space into two equal halves in which the large pool to the left seems in balance with the small pool and raised dining terrace on the right.

Asymmetry can also be balanced If you lay out each element so that it's a mirror image of another element, decision making becomes easier. Everything matches. The only problem is that a symmetrical arrangement can sometimes seem completely predictable. One antidote is to create asymmetrical spaces on either side of something central, combining visual interest with clarity of intent.

Maverick that I am, I tend to want to break symmetry as soon as I see it, yet at the same time keep garden elements in balance. The way I do it is to keep something aligned, such as a pathway to the house, but place the elements around it asymmetrically, such as trees, shrubs, and planting beds. I'll discuss placement of objects in more detail in the chapter "Placing the Pieces" on p. 168.

On the Angle

In an On the Angle arrangement, diagonal lines shift the axis of a space off center and have the benefit of energizing, elongating, and expanding the landscape. A diagonal is the straight line that joins opposite corners of a rectangle or a square; it's the lon-

ALL-LINED UP VS. ON THE ANGLE

A side yard with four trees set around a square patio is all-lined up and balanced.

The same side yard with three different-size trees and a patio at an angle to the house is on an angle but it still feels balanced and complete.

gest side of a right triangle (the hypotenuse). From a bird's-eye perspective, a diagonal cuts obliquely across the ground plane, forcing the eye (and the feet, if it's a path) to move all the way to the corners and making a landscape seem much bigger than it really is.

We're used to seeing things neatly squared up in the backyard, with patios, planting beds, lawns, and vegetable gardens all lined up, but you'll begin to look differently at your property if you introduce some diagonals. You can get a sense of the powerful energy of a diagonal line simply by moving furniture inside or outside your house. Set your living room couch on the diagonal and see how it changes the dynamics of the room. Then move outside and place an outdoor dining set so that it's on a 45-degree angle to a square deck, and you'll start to see your backyard in a new light. Although diagonal lines may not be suited to every space, it's a good idea to try to incorporate some diagonal element into your home outside.

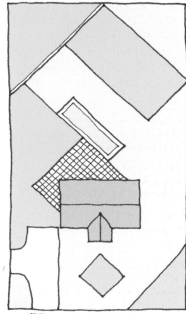

ON THE ANGLE

This terrace lies "on the angle" in relation to the wall that shelters it from neighboring views. The juxtaposition of angles gives an energy and expansiveness to this small property in Los Angeles.

(far left) Twin curving staircases connect a formal upper terrace to a more informal lower garden in an urban backyard the author designed some years ago. White redbud trees arch above a marble figure that matches the statue in the cavelike grotto across the way.

(left) The elegant curving line that forms the banks of this pond signals that it was created by the hand of humans, not by nature.

Voluptuous Curves

When I have a hard time convincing clients to let me create the sweeping arcs, spirals, and semicircles that I love, I simply tell them, "I'd like to create some curves—voluptuous curves." That word usually does the trick.

Why is the idea of a voluptuous curve so appealing? I think it goes back to our time as infants, when we nestled within the enclosing arms of our mothers. A mother's body serves as a child's first landscape—a home, a haven, a harbor. So it may be that shapes that swell, curves that contain, and lines that carve out space delight us on some deep and subconscious level.

But it's not just the shape of the human body that offers inspiration for making voluptuous curves. Think of the beauty of an oxbow of a river, the meander of a stream, the inward-curving eddies found in the lee of a stone caught in a rushing brook. Studying the movement of liquid through such watercourses can teach you how to draw the beautiful line on your land. The Japanese did just that: Young designers would trek into nature to study streambeds, islands, waterfalls, and other landforms. Then they returned to their cramped cities and, in the tiny spaces available to them, re-created abstracted versions of the beauty they found in nature. They'd forget the scruffy underbrush and plant the pure form of a mossy bank. Mentally they would remove the detritus, twigs, and froth from a natural watercourse and re-create its graceful sweeps and curves, carving out channels that looked like commas or apostrophes—reversing the curves so they flowed sinuously down a hill to a pool.

(facing page) Made of long slabs of concrete, this walkway is designed to move through the diminutive backyard on an angle, but it also uses diminishing perspective to carve out space and seem much longer than it really is.

VOLUPTUOUS CURVES

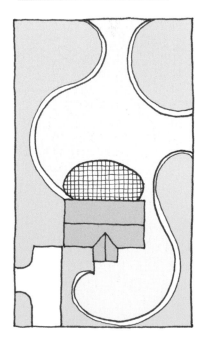

BIG MOVES IN SMALL PLACES

You don't need a huge property to combine big moves in interesting ways. A client of ours had a wonderful lakefront property, but it looked right down on the next-door neighbor. We combined artful screening to set off a landscape that combines all three types of aesthetic arrangements in a very small space. The garden itself is All Lined Up on the living-room windows, with a Voluptuous Curving circular path around the perimeter that intersects with two crossing paths On the Angle.

Just as you can combine layouts in your landscape, you can also use different arrangements on the same property. For instance, if you chose Open-Air Rooms as your layout, each of the rooms could be organized with a particular arrangement. Or, if you live in a forest and chose the Immersed layout, you could still arrange the sitting areas under the trees so that one is On the Angle, another All Lined Up, and yet another designed with Voluptuous Curves. The possibilities are endless.

You can transform a small backyard into a private oasis with a tall hedge to block your neighbors and a few big moves.

(far left) A grass path set between curvilinear planting beds winds its way back into space.

(left) Seen from above, the curved walls around this circular terrace are just the right height for sitting—about 15 inches. This cut-granite patio is created by using larger stones at the perimeter and ever smaller stones toward the center.

THE BEAUTY OF CURVES

When I'm trying to make my point to a client about the beauty of curves, I'll grab a rake or shovel, or even a stick, to draw a sinewy line upon the earth. Sometimes I use a hose or a rope to express the elegance of an S-curve. Lately, I've taken to keeping cans of orange biodegradable spray paint in my car for just this purpose. I love to draw out the unfurling of a fern frond, the inward spiraling of a path up to the top of a mount, or the location of a pinched "waist" in a walkway, like an hourglass shape on the land. No matter what kind of garden I'm designing, my perpetual quest is to find the beautiful line.

It's hard to resist the attraction of a sinuous gravel path that snakes its way through a lush landscape.

Curves stand in stark contrast to the buildings that define their edges. Walls that rise high and run straight usually protect the garden from the street. These gardens, then, are bounded by architecture on all sides, enclosed by straight lines that define the garden space. Within the leftover, often rectangular space, curves feel wonderfully right to the viewer, in part because they relate to those found in nature and in part because they offer such a stark contrast to the strict linear geometry of their setting. These voluptuous curves are the yin of nature that completes the yang of the architecture.

Identify a Theme

Once you've selected your preferred layout and chosen one or more aesthetic arrangements, you can go one step further and identify a theme. You don't have to select a theme for your landscape to look good: Choosing a layout and an arrangement will bring coherence to your design thinking without it. But if you are able to come up with a distinctive theme, you'll find yourself thinking about the design of your property in a whole new way.

Identifying a particular theme is the hardest and most interesting part of any design process. A theme is a unifying idea or quality that sets it apart from other properties around it, no matter how big or how small it might be. Even if you live in a row house or a cottage, you can pick a theme or concept that expresses who you are and how you choose to live on your land. The subject matter can come from your own background or personality, your family's interests or traditions, or something special about your property, neighborhood, or region. Remind yourself of some of these ideas by going back over the work you did in the chapter "The Lay of the Land" on p. 20. Now we get to apply this information to help create a truly distinctive design for your landscape.

What's the advantage of finding a theme for your property? Coming up with an image of what you want to create there will help you define both big moves and small, down to the finest details. Let me explain. My husband and I bought a house in the country a few years ago. While we were renovating the house, we spent a lot of time outdoors removing dead trees and invasive species from our land. All this time, we were searching for the right theme for our property. Developed by the previous owner as a large Central Clearing, our landscape includes an open field and a swimming pond, surrounded by forest. Moose, coyote, fox, deer, beaver, and wild turkey are common visitors, as are the porcupines that come by each evening. Thanks to them and the rolling land we live on, we've come to call our property "Porcupine Paradise."

Along with the name comes an implicit vision: to maintain our property as a wildlife haven to keep the critters safe and our porcupines coming back. Also implied in our vision is a sense of how to develop the land further: We are making simple gardens just around the house, but farther out, we've chosen to leave the land as natural

(above) An Arts and Crafts-style house relates beautifully to its curvilinear landscape.

(right) Name that theme: This play space in a small urban backyard calls to mind the image of a tree house in an island jungle.

as possible, editing it to maintain diverse habitats for the wildlife by mowing fields, hacking back invasives, and—as necessary—logging the woodlands that surround us. The name Porcupine Paradise gives rise to our mutual vision to keep our property a safe zone for wildlife.

There are a number of ways to identify a theme for your property: Determining Your Style, Naming the Property, or Dreaming the Big Idea. Each strategy can organize your design thinking in a whole new way.

Determining Your Style

To help determine your style, ask yourself if there is any particular overriding look that fits your image for your landscape. Just as your house may have been built in a specific style—an English Tudor or a Cape, for example—your landscape can take on a style as well. It could be a historical style such as Arts and Crafts, Victorian, Early American, or Modernist, to name a few. Or it could be a cultural or geographical style such as Japanese, Mexican, or Southwestern. It could also be a style derived from the house and its setting, such as a Cabin in the Woods, a Hunting Lodge, a Farmhouse, or a Tropical Paradise. Each of these suggests a different way to lay out, design, and even decorate your landscape.

Giving Your Property a Name

Another way to identify your property's theme is to give it a name. What would you call the place where you live? Friends of mine who live in Maine named their home on a sliver of land "Tight Squeeze." Like their property, their house is unusually narrow and long, with a terrace and play area shoehorned in to fit. Similarly, a great-aunt of mine called her place "Rosecroft." She had lived in an apartment house most of her

(above left) This Italian-style garden used to be a parking lot covered in asphalt. The owners wanted the new landscape to relate to the architecture of the historic Italianate house.

(above right) The historic or cultural backdrop of the region you live in can help you identify a theme. Here, the southwestern landscape melds contemporary versions of traditional adobe-style architecture with brightly colored plantings that tolerate dry conditions, known as xeriscaping.

When you name your house and garden, you give visitors a sense of what to expect when they arrive at your doorstep. The name of this rusty red house with a creeping thyme terrace is *Chili Rojo*, which means "red chile."

life, moving into a tiny cottage in a retirement village near the end of her life. Thrilled to have a little front garden for the first time, she filled it with scented climbers, rosebushes, and feeders for the birds.

Another friend longed to return to her roots where she grew up on a farm in the Midwest. But she lived on a small in-town lot. So she decided to call her yard "The Back Forty," and then developed a small vegetable garden, an apiary, and a diminutive orchard there. A name can suggest an appropriate organizing strategy that might inform what you choose to do there. For example, a friend and her husband call their property "Evernest," where they are building a series of little huts, cabins, and special destinations for family and friends.

Naming helps you establish a theme that will provide an underlying blueprint for the way you develop your property in the future. Sometimes a characteristic of the area or region you live in will suggest the theme (like Porcupine Paradise). Sometimes an attribute, style, or feature of your house will give a clue (like Tight Squeeze), or a particular landscape or garden highlight from your experience will surface as a theme you'd like to develop on your land (like Rosecroft or The Back Forty).

Dreaming the Big Idea

Identifying a theme can go even further than choosing a style or naming your property. The very best landscapes are those that have what I call a "Big Idea"—an organizing concept that helps you determine many of the design decisions thereafter.

The most important work I do for my clients is to come up with the Big Idea that holds their design together and makes it unique. The idea can come from just about anywhere—a remark they made, a painting on their wall, a particular tree in their backyard, the curve of a hillside in the distance. I've designed landscapes based on a favorite children's book, a painting, a piece of music, or even the shape of a flower or a butterfly. Sometimes the idea comes to me in the middle of the night or when brainstorming with my colleagues in the studio. What I've learned is that this galvanizing idea is necessary for us to take a design to a level higher than just solving problems. It's the place where artistry comes into play.

A Big Idea can be one grand schema or superstructure that informs every decision thereafter or a series of "Little Big Ideas," each of which has its own integrity. Either way, getting to the Big Idea—"dreaming" it—is the most fun work we do. When we get it right, everyone knows it and it's easy to move forward from there. Being able to come up with such a defining concept is at the core of the creative process. You know it when you see—or dream—it.

One way to dream up the Big Idea is to ask, "What if?" For instance, we might ask, "What if we turned that drainage swale into a dry streambed?" Or "What if that stairway looked like a waterfall?" A designer friend, who designed a garden for a tall couple, asked herself, "What if their landscape were the same scale as they are?" She ended up creating a bold garden full of high plantings, large sculptures, and overscaled furniture. (Privately, she referred to it as "The Land of the Giants!")

(above) This unique, renovated landscape goes by the mysterious name of the Garden of Elegant Ruin. The crumbling retaining wall was restored with aqueduct-like arches housing nooks, shelves, and a water wall. Plant leaves pressed into the drying concrete reinforce the historic feeling.

(left) "Little Big Ideas" can be very personal. Here, the owners planted four crabapple trees in this wildflower meadow, one for each of their sons.

A GRANDCHILD'S PARADISE

Sometimes, the Big Idea comes out of an emotion—in this case, out of love. When my parents retired, they moved north to an old farmhouse perched on the shores of the Connecticut River. The land was overgrown with brambles, but they set to work, clearing it to make a unique landscape. Their vision was to make a grandchild's paradise full of spaces so special that each child would delight in spending much of his or her summer there.

And that is just what happened. With this idea in mind, they created a family gathering place that all 22 grandchildren love to visit. There's swimming, boating, and games for active play but also a playhouse, a gazebo, a hammock, and a tree house. And then there are the personal touches that are strewn throughout the landscape: the giant rusting dragon, the wooden cutouts of beloved family cats and dogs in the pet

cemetery, the birdhouses painted by the grandchildren, the fire pit for family sing-alongs.

Over the years, I've watched my parents change the landscape to suit their fancy or their physical condition or to try out something new. The place feels like it's always the same yet somehow always changing. It is a place for lasting memories—truly a grandchild's paradise.

[1] A giant rusting dragon dominates the lawn, with the children's playhouse ("Netherby") observing from a safe distance.

[2] Now that's a flower bed!

[3] The rose tunnel.

[4] Handprints and names set in the garden steps immortalize each of the grandchildren.

One Landscape,

While making the Big Moves may be one of the most challenging parts of the design process, it's also the most fun because when you choose a layout, select an arrangement, and identify a theme, you begin to give real form to your landscape. As you work through this process, don't forget to take out your tracing paper and sketch out your ideas, making overlays as you go. Try different combinations—a Central Clearing set On the Angle, for instance, or Open-Air Rooms that are made up of

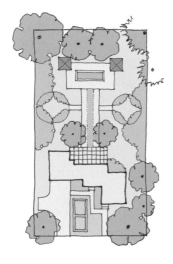

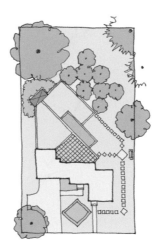

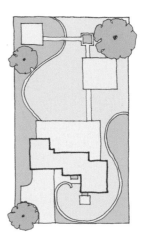

The Orderly Garden

This is the landscape for someone who likes symmetry and formality. In the backyard, every move is a mirror of each other. The surprise is the formal but asymmetrical front yard.

- **Layout:** House Front and Center
- **Arrangement:** All Lined Up
- **Big Idea:** Almost Perfect Symmetry

The Diagonal Garden

Here, paths and places are developed around diagonal movement. The square turned on end in the front yard gives the first clue. The second clue is the terrace and reflecting pool, both set on an angle to the house and giving rise to the location of the paths and a grove of trees set on the diagonal.

- **Layout:** Exposed
- **Arrangement:** On the Angle
- **Big Idea:** Diagonal Movement

The Garden of Voluptuous Curves

Both the name and the design of this landscape show the effect of Voluptuous Curves that start at the front door and curve back around both sides of the property, creating an elegant Central Clearing.

- **Layout:** Central Clearing
- **Arrangement:** Voluptuous Curves
- **Big Idea:** A Lyrical Landscape

Six Possibilities

Voluptuous Curves. Then, if you have identified a theme, trace out what it might mean in terms of form.

As a summary of the design ideas presented in this chapter, take a look at the six landscape designs below. Each of the designs was created for the same simple property, using a different set of Big Moves. Try this yourself on your own site plan. You'll be amazed at how quickly you can create completely different designs for your property.

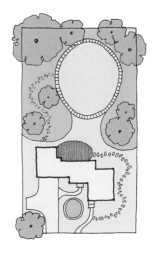

The Elliptical Garden

In this garden we played with oval forms, using them as a garden pool in the front yard and as the shape for a platform or terrace and a lawn panel, both in the backyard. Repeating these forms brings a unity to the whole property.

- **Layout:** Immersed or Exposed
- **Arrangement:** Voluptuous Curves
- **Big Idea:** Repeating Ovals

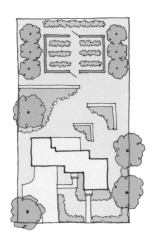

The Garden of Enclosing Arms

In this garden, we played with some of the energy principles that are discussed later: ripple effect (see p. 192) and receiving forms (see p. 198), which are both seen in the angled walls in the backyard. A formal vegetable garden sits at the back of the site.

- **Layout:** Open-Air Rooms
- **Arrangement:** On the Angle
- **Big Idea:** Energy

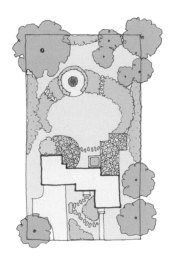

Party Central

The Big Idea of this landscape was simply to have a good time on the different terraces and around the fire pit.

- **Layout:** Central Clearing
- **Arrangement:** Voluptuous Curves
- **Big Idea:** Party Central

LIVING ALFRESCO

This tight San Francisco lot with neighbors on all sides packs a bundle of Big Moves into a tiny space. Landscape designer Alma Hecht turned a formal Italianate garden into a casual landscape for celebrations, hands-on gardening, and quiet contemplation for her client, a busy executive with a culinary background and a love of good wines. In the 30-ft. by 100-ft. backyard, Alma deftly combined an Immersed layout with Open-Air Rooms, all organized around a path that's On the Angle.

The Big Idea came when Alma realized that her client's home was just too small to contain all his passions, so she moved some of the inside home *outside*. She designed a "dining room" with a beach glass mosaic–topped table for eight and a "bottle wall" built of wine bottles on concrete shelves. The "den" has a "ceiling" of twisting grapevines that grow over metal stalks with bulb tops. It is furnished with a couch and two chairs around a square fire pit, with a floor of blue-toned river rock. Other rooms include a so-called

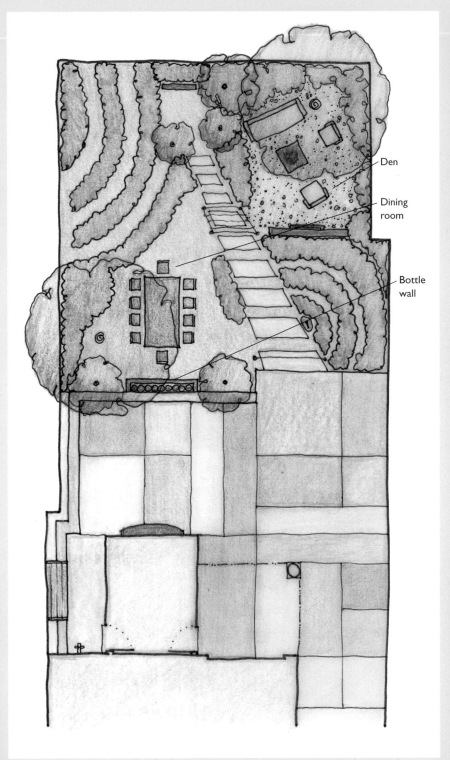

Den

Dining room

Bottle wall

1 Handcrafted metal sculptures flank an entry path of stones cut on the angle that lead in ever-decreasing sizes to a mirrored door at the far end of the property.

2 Designer Alma Hecht hand-fabricated the mosaic grapevine table that seats up to eight.

3 A wall of wine bottles combines visual interest with translucent screening.

"Scentual Garden," located behind the dining room, where it takes advantage of the southern sunlight. It is planted with curving beds of roses and other plants for cutting. At the head of the "horizon path" is the herb/lettuce patch, complete with a sundial, which is separated from the den by a concrete growing wall. At its terminus sits the "horizon door," with mirrors to give the illusion of more space.

Gateways created from hand-sculpted metal ornamental onions flank the skewed cut-stone pathway, continuing as a metal, vine-covered arbor that opens onto the den. To screen the tall apartment house next door, Alma planted fast-growing trees, and a freestanding wall to the west blocks the winds that whip down the driveway.

Her delighted client has the following to say about his space: "I love that the garden is divided into many different areas. It feels so spacious and yet so private. From cutting flowers in the Scentual Garden, to drinks and dinner in the dining room, or curled up in the den by the fire with a good book, it's as if the garden can respond to whatever mood I might be in."

1 This tiny San Francisco backyard is truly a home outside, complete with a dining room, a cozy nook, and a corridor that links the two together.

2 The fire pit in the "den."

Comfort Zones

*"Everyone can identify with a fragrant garden,
with the beauty of sunset, with the quiet of nature,
with a warm and cozy cottage."*

—THOMAS KINKADE

Wherever you live, whether in a country cottage, a suburban ranch, a multiunit townhouse, or a fifth-floor walk-up, the space around your dwelling should feel like a zone of comfort in your everyday world. It's the front yard that you walk through as you leave for work in the morning and return to with a deep sigh of relief at the end of a long day. It's the backyard where you take your ease in a hammock, dip your hands into the earth to plant a bulb, or breathe in the fresh smell of cut grass on a lazy Saturday afternoon. It's the getaway zone at the edge of the property where your children build forts, climb trees, or hide under bushes, safe and secure on your land. For it's not just your house that provides a sense of security from the world outside its walls, but it's also the landscape around it that offers reassurance and brings a sense of ease into your life.

WHAT DO WE MEAN BY COMFORT ZONES?

Comfort zones are the different areas around the house that provide the conditions in which a homeowner can feel physically and mentally relaxed. Depending on the location of the zone (front, side, or back of the house); the size of the property; the particular preferences of the homeowner; and the relationship to neighbors, these conditions may vary.

Everyone's definition of comfort is a little different from his or her neighbors'. Yet there are some general perspectives and rules of thumb that you can apply to your own property to make the zones around your house work better for you and your family. That's what this chapter is all about.

Once you've come to know your actual and ideal sites (see pp. 20–49) and decided on the big moves (pp. 50–83) you can begin the design process in earnest. You start to define how the different zones on your property can create a sense of comfort for you and your family. In this chapter, you'll learn to map out the relationships between your house and landscape, the front and back, and your property and its surrounding neighborhood. I use bubble diagrams to sketch out these interrelationships to understand how best to organize the many types of spaces and their uses, both inside and outside the house.

There are four kinds of comfort zones related to the home outside. There's the Surrounding Zone—the broad area around your property that influences the way you live there; the Welcoming Zone—the front of your property where visitors approach to enter; the Neighboring Zone—the perimeter of your property where you can choose the degree of enclosure you'd prefer; and the Living Zone—the areas inside and outside the house where you can create gathering, getaway, and play spaces

(right) The tiniest urban backyard can still feel like a woodsy refuge. By planting just two or three small ornamental shade trees around a terrace, you create a verdant canopy overhead.

(below) When you live in a woodland setting, a clearing becomes a comfort zone because it brings sunlight and air circulation to an otherwise dark, dank space. This homeowner cleared a small area to build a simple house in the woods and installed a pond that reflects the sky.

for you and your family. The right layout for each one of these four zones contributes mightily to the overall sense of comfort—and pleasure—that you feel when you step onto your property. After all, being "in your comfort zone" is more than just an expression; it's really the definition of home. Let's examine each zone.

The Surrounding Zone

No matter where your property is—city, suburb, or country—it is part of a larger context. It belongs to a surrounding region, a local community, a particular neighborhood, each a part of what constitutes "home." It's useful to think broadly about the larger context in which your property sits. The geologic makeup of the region, its history, and the neighborhood setting all affect the way you inhabit your land. When you learn about your property's background, you'll have a clearer understanding of how your design fits into the fabric of the whole.

Your backyard does not have to be one large open "great room" but can be composed of smaller "rooms" along a grassy "hallway" that links them together.

BUILDING ON THE PAST

It can be fascinating to look into the history of your surrounding area to determine who lived there before you and how the community you live in developed over time. In my case, we live in a town settled before the Revolutionary War. Our house is up a long dirt road, on the site of a hunting cabin, next to a byway traveled by stagecoaches in the mid-1800s. Remnants of old structures dot the landscape, as do ancient apple trees near the site of a long-lost house foundation. The first settlers here probably raised sheep on this land, which explains the old animal runs and stone walls, often topped with barbed wire nailed into what are now aged oak trees.

Knowing its history changes the way we live on this land. We planted new apple trees to augment those by the old homestead. We mowed grass paths through the hayfields to take our visitors to the historic areas on our property. We've cleared the ground around the old structures and foundations to make the site's history more visible to us on a daily basis. Knowing your area's past brings the satisfaction of being part of a historic continuum, while providing insights into how to properly develop its future.

The immediate neighborhood around your house is an important comfort zone. Sharing safe and people-friendly streets, sidewalks, and parks helps us live happily while in community with others.

The geologic and hydrologic history of the ground beneath your house predates it by millions of years. Whether glaciers scraped across the land, ancient sea or lake beds left their mark, or the land perches by the edge of an ocean all influence the design decisions you may choose to make. My old house sat on a high bluff that was thought to have been formed by an ancient fault line that may have been one of the points where the supercontinent of Pangaea divided into tectonic plates. My children and I found it exciting to think that our land sat at the very spot where Africa and America were joined 180 million years ago, and we created a little stone terrace as a contemplative overlook there to celebrate it.

Not only your site's natural history affects how you live on your land but also its climate, hydrology, ecology, and even soil structure. If you live in Hurricane Alley, for example, you'll choose building and plant materials differently than if you live in a less wind-prone climate. If you reside on the site of a prehistoric lake, you'll find that

THE SURROUNDING ZONE

Home is not just the four walls of your house but also the larger context in which it sits. Your town, your neighborhood, and the street where you live are all a part of "home."

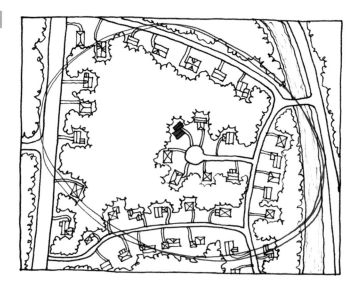

your soils are composed of sand and silt that may need to be enriched for any gardening you choose to do.

The community and amenities in which your property is located have a big impact on the way you live there. But neighborhood satisfaction is hard to measure. Think about all the features that you and your family enjoy in your area, including the schools, libraries, and parks in your community, and its ball fields, trails, natural areas, picnic shelters, greenways, shade trees, playgrounds, vacant lots, and pools. More intangible amenities include qualities like a network of safe and walkable streets, a viable center and edge, a diversity of houses, and the availability of public transportation. Each of these contributes to your sense of your neighborhood's livability, which in turn affects your satisfaction with your home, your community, and your life in general.

Your Surrounding Zone is full of rich and satisfying places that have meaning for you and your loved ones. These special places supplement the qualities found on your property and extend the presence of home out into the community itself. Once

SPECIAL PLACES

A fun thing to do with your family is to ask each member to list his or her special places, both on and off your property. Each holds a particular meaning for the person who remembers them. Your memory is chock full of such sites, and it's interesting once in a while to share this information and appreciate them anew.

A few members of our family came up with the following list of special places in and around the upper Connecticut River Valley area of New Hampshire.

Special Activities near our home:

Natural places
- tubing on the White River
- taking visitors to Quechee Gorge
- hikes on Ascutney Mountain
- party barging on the Connecticut River
- running down the "Dirtiest Place in the World"

Sports Activities
- football games at Dartmouth
- ice skating on Storrs Pond
- cross country skiing on Oak Hill
- sledding at the Country Club

Cultural Activities
- Montshire Museum
- concerts at Hopkins Center
- exhibits at Hood Museum
- bonfires at Winter Carnival

Special Events
- Shriner's Parade
- Big Apple Circus

Farms, Gardens and Food
- strawberry picking
- The Dairy Twirl
- farmers' markets
- Dirt Cowboy Café

If you live in the mountains, you'll probably want to feature a long view across a valley to the peaks beyond. This New York property is part of the Hudson Highlands and is covered with quartzite, a metamorphic rock.

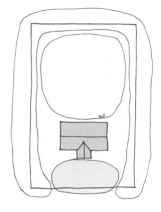

you've thought about the area surrounding your land, you can turn your eyes to the property itself and consider the zone that deals with the entrance to the property, the area I call the Welcoming Zone.

The Welcoming Zone

When it comes to our homes, most of us would like to show a welcoming face to the world. We'd like our visitors to feel that we're glad they've come—and that once they enter, they will be graciously received. We also want to create a home that feels welcoming to family members and to ourselves. When we drive into the garage after a hard day's work, we want to feel relieved that we've arrived home. When kids come home from college, we want them to feel delighted that they've returned. The front of a property acts as the gateway to one's house—the Welcoming Zone that invites entry and gives a hint as to who lives inside.

(above) When you live in an apartment, you're thrilled to share a bit of ground, even when it's in the front yard. This building does everything it can to seem welcoming, down to the placement of the Adirondack chairs either side of the front door.

(right) Concrete pavers spill forward amongst the plants to welcome visitors to this contemporary California home.

(facing page) This charming home is named Lavender House, not only for its color but also for the scent of the herb by that name. It is one in a larger community of small houses whose front facade clearly welcomes visitors in but whose back enjoys complete privacy.

How welcoming is your front yard? Pretend you're a visitor arriving at your home for the first time. Go outside and walk the route that a car would take to enter your property. Then walk it again, from the point of view of the passerby. What do you see? Most likely, the first thing you encounter is the driveway.

Designing Driveways

Unless you live in an urban location, the first time you visit someone, you probably drive to get there. When you think about it, your driveway and parking area are really the front walk and welcome mat for the car. As such, their design matters. Notice where your driveway leads. Does it direct you to the front door? The back door? Do you need to walk a long way to get there? Or is your front door also your back door? There are many different ways to design this Welcoming Zone, but some work better than others. Let's look at a few of these driveway options: the circular driveway, the drive court, and the hammerhead.

You can design your front yard for privacy, even in a close-knit suburban location. A low wall bisects the land in front of this home into a handsome entry court and a more sheltered garden around the house.

This attractive curved driveway is composed of two permeable surfaces: loose gravel for the tire tracks and a grassy strip down the middle, with the whole edged by lawn. A well-draining surface like this does not require a drainage ditch to either side, as more impervious surfaces do.

A circular driveway is good at getting guests right to the front door, making it an excellent choice for ease of access for the elderly, disabled, or people with young children. On the downside, it requires two curb cuts, takes up most of a typical front yard, and can leave behind an underdeveloped semicircular island along the street. A drive court is a good choice for a front yard that has the space along its side to handle it. While it doesn't lead directly to the front entryway as the circular driveway does, the drive court provides parking for a large group of cars along the property line, hidden by walls, fences, or hedges. The hammerhead driveway is the most utilitarian configuration of the three and takes up the least amount of space in the front yard, but it also gives the least amount of parking area. One advantage over a straight driveway is that a hammerhead allows you to make a three-point turn rather than backing straight out into the street.

THREE DRIVEWAYS

Circular driveway

Drive court

Hammerhead driveway

(above left) The white gravel of the driveway matches the color of the house, and the whole is carefully edged in stone, helping it feel clearly defined yet welcoming.

(above right) Concrete pavers can make an appealing drive court on a small site. Choose the color, texture, and size carefully for ease of maintenance (and ease of shoveling in winter) to harmonize with the colors of the house and garage. Soften the edges with plantings and, as in this case, an attractive entry fence.

DID YOU KNOW?

Using an environmentally responsible driveway material, such as recycled rubber tires mixed with peastone and bound together by resins, allows water to drain through the driveway surface.

The Garage at the Center

In many newly developed properties, the first thing you see is the garage. To minimize the amount of driveway and maximize backyard space, many builders pull the garage forward of the plane of the house so that the garage doors face you as you enter. For a visitor, this is not only disconcerting but also disorienting: Where should you park your car—in front of the garage where it might block your hosts or in the hammerhead space where they make their turn? Both are bad options. And how should you enter the house—through the garage or somewhere around the side of the house where you hope to find a front door? How can you provide your visitor with a more welcoming first experience of your home?

One solution is to make the garage itself more welcoming. You can build a pergola over the garage doors and plant trailing vines over it, dressing it up so that it looks more presentable as one's first view of your house. Another solution, especially where space is at a premium, is to segment a narrow driveway into one area for "visitor parking" and another as a paved entry walk. Minimizing the drive area and setting it off with a different material than the front walk calls attention to the surface underfoot, rather than to the yawning maw of the garage doors. You can also find ways to visually screen the garage area with trees and shrubs by making a drive court for guests that sits close to the front door.

ADDING A PERGOLA

Building a pergola over the garage that connects to the front entrance makes the entry more welcoming and deemphasizes the blank wall of the garage door.

(left) This garage greets you as you turn into the driveway, but the continuity of materials encourages you to follow a path that takes you to the backyard sitting area. Without the soft billow of plantings at its base, the effect would be entirely different.

(below) This garage is detailed and decorated just like the house it is attached to. Although it juts forward from the house, it is turned 90 degrees and feels well nestled into a lush planting bed.

GARAGE MAKEOVER

The owner of this tired old garage wanted to focus on gardening as her passion in retirement. A plain stucco garage, long ignored, received a second wind when Mary Dewart of Dewart Design re-created the building as a retreat and play space for the homeowner.

The existing garage was dominated by a wide asphalt driveway, a burned-out lawn, and a large, overgrown tree. The tree trunk abutted the garage, leaning precariously over the structure. It was a difficult decision to make, but Mary and the client knew that the tree had to come down. She also took up the driveway and transformed much of the lawn into cheerful perennial beds.

This project illustrates many of the spatial vantage points described on pp. 45–47. In creating the various landscaped spaces around the property, Mary added an elevated deck (a "promontory") near the entry steps and an "island" flower bed. The retreat's interior is a "cave" for the lucky owner and visitors, while outside, a gravel and stepping-stone sitting area serves as a "harbor" where one can relax, protected, while enjoying the view to the surrounding gardens.

The converted garage serves as part gardening shed, part writer's studio, and part getaway escape from which to view the new perennial beds.

If you are building a brand-new house, make sure your garage doesn't take center stage in the Welcoming Zone. One way to do this is to turn the garage away from the house, so that it opens to the side of the property, not the front. You can also set the front face of the garage back several feet from the house front so that it isn't on the same plane as the front door but steps back from it. If you can live without an attached garage, the simplest way to de-emphasize a garage on your property is to banish it to the back of the lot, where it can serve as an all-in-one tool shed, storage facility, and basketball stand.

Front Yards

Besides the driveway, the other important Welcoming Zone is the front yard, the ground in front of the house that offers guests their first visual experience of your property. It can also tell visitors something about your personality as a homeowner and give a clue as to how welcoming a person you are.

(above) A charming shrub border embraces a pair of comfortable chairs resting on a small patio tucked below the bay window, providing a personal touch to an otherwise "democratic front lawn."

(below) Even the tiniest front yard can reveal something about the homeowner's personality. In this Washington, D.C., neighborhood, a formally sheared boxwood garden stands in stark contrast to the free-form cottage garden next door.

Seeding in a wildflower lawn to replace Kentucky bluegrass can be an easy-care, soft-to-the-touch front-yard solution. Best of all, the right species require little or no watering once they're established.

Deeply ingrained within the American psyche is a stereotype I call "the democratic front lawn." This type of lawn is a perfectly manicured swath of open turf that starts at the street and sweeps back, carpetlike, up to the traditional foundation plantings that skirt the house. It's democratic because everyone can see it all—there's no place to hide—yet somehow there is no display of unfettered free expression—everyone conforms to the standard lawn and foundation-planting solution. Thus, many front yards give passersby little information about the people who live there. With the size of lots shrinking, it may be time to rethink what we do with this important zone of our house. (It's not unlike the unused space inside many oversized houses—the formal dining room that rarely sees diners or the massive great room that is shunned in favor of a cozier den.) Leaving the front yard as a bland, useless space is a waste of resources and ingenuity and certainly doesn't foster a sense of neighborliness.

In many developments, the color chosen for the front door or the window trim is the only thing that sets one home apart from another. But visit the backyard and

RETHINKING THE FRONT YARD

With just a few changes to the planting scheme, a new home in an exposed bulldozed lot can soon feel settled into its neighborhood. Two birches set in soft meadow grasses veil the house and provide foreground interest to the site.

you'll experience something entirely different. Here, the homeowners let their guard down, displaying their personality and setting themselves off as different from their neighbors. Perhaps we're all afraid of what people will think, so we hide our real selves in the backyard. Many of us seem to have no idea what to do as an alternative to the democratic front lawn; take a look at the photos on pp. 100–101 for some front-yard inspiration.

Think of your front yard as a backyard The best way to treat a front yard is just as you'd treat the backyard. Plant it, personalize it, and enjoy it just as though it were hidden from your neighbors' views. Show it off and enjoy the compliments. Even relax and entertain there, making the most of every square inch of the property that you're lucky enough to steward.

When you take away the neighborhood (or personal) strictures about what a front yard "should" look like and think of it as though it's a backyard, you may be

Celebrate the unusual in your own front yard. With an eye-popping statue, assorted bird-houses, architectural details, and favorite plants, there's nothing too predictable about this front garden.

MAKING THE MOST OF YOUR FRONT YARD

With space around our houses at a premium, it pays to make the most of your front yard, both as a way to showcase your house and to use as a Welcoming Zone for sitting, gathering, or gardening.

1 A townhouse front yard.

2 Matching seat covers to plantings shows a keen attention to detail.

3 A front lawn of meadow grasses.

4 A neighborly spot for after-noon tea.

5 A bungalow accessed by a winding front walk.

6 The narrow front yard accommodates an entry walk and a meandering gravel path through a garden.

7 An arbor over the front walk shows the way to the front door.

8 A colorful house deserves a brightly hued planting.

9 The red picket fence that encloses the yard picks up the trim color of the house.

surprised at how valuable it suddenly becomes. For instance, there's no reason you can't create a space for sitting there. Why not place pots, statues, bird feeders, or hanging baskets out for your visitors and neighbors to enjoy? And why not enclose the front yard so that it feels protected, just as the backyard does? It's exciting to imagine the possibilities that come from reframing your image of what a front yard can be.

Yard as garden The original definition of "yard" is an area of land where animals were penned. Most likely, this is not the image that you wish to convey to your guests. Instead, think of your front yard as a front garden—a handsome showplace of trees, shrubs, flowers, and focal points, set out for the enjoyment of yourselves and others.

You might begin by cutting some appealing patterns into that perfect lawn and planting these beds with your favorite flowers. Make crescents, ovals, S-curves, spirals, or simple straight rows. These beds can border the front walk or take the place of

A handsome picket fence surrounds a "door-yard" garden that visitors walk through to get to the front door. At the corner, a weeping cherry tree provides an appropriate scale against the low-slung roof of this Ohio house.

ho-hum foundation plantings. You might decide to expand your design· making a formal parterre of clipped hedges, a rockery of alpine plantings, or a cheerful cottage garden that fills the whole front yard. Think about leaving a space for a bench, a chaise longue, or a grassy circle where you can place a table and chairs.

The use of focal points can enhance the interest of your front yard as well as reveal a little of your personality to your neighbors. Over the years, I've amassed a host of personal objects—an antique metal knight who guards the house, an Austrian bell, ornate stone planters, concrete animals collected by my kids—that adorn the front stoop and door where I live. I've seen others place statuary, sundials, and cascading fountains in their front yard, turning it into a garden for all to enjoy.

Since most front yards are so exposed to the street, it's important that what you plant matches the style of your house. A Georgian colonial may look best with formal hedges and symmetrical plantings. A little bungalow can nestle happily within a whirl of cottage-garden plantings. A low-slung modernist home can stand up to the

(left) A wildflower meadow nearly engulfs this one-story contemporary home, backed up by a belt of trees.

(below left) When you live at the corner of a busy street, a hedge across your front porch acts as a screen from oncoming headlights and the curiosity of passersby. Widening the planting bed at the corner and placing an edging of cobblestones between plantings and lawn give something back to those who walk and drive by.

(below right) Plantings in muted shades of green, red, and earth tones blend beautifully with the colors of the house.

abstract lines of a Japanese-style garden or the billows of a prairie garden. Make sure to echo the colors, textures, and materials of your house and garden.

Front Porches

In the days before computers, television, and other in-home distractions, front stoops and porches were important gathering spaces in a close-knit neighborhood. On summer nights, homeowners would gather to enjoy the twilight hours or cool evening breezes after sundown, calling out to neighbors to stop by and sit awhile on a wicker rocker or porch swing.

In today's fast-paced, plugged-in world, a front porch can still be an informal gathering space or getaway zone—a cozy outdoor living space from where you can look out over both front yard and neighborhood streetscape. If you decorate the porch with favorite potted plants, comfortable furniture, carpets, and wall hangings, you'll find yourself sitting out there at all times of the day—to watch the sunrise with

If a front porch is deep enough, it can double as an outdoor family room. This porch swing provides a quiet place for two just off the main living spaces of the house.

a steaming cup of coffee in hand, enjoy a quick lunch on the porch, or sit out after dinner for a quiet moment before turning in for the night. A front porch, while reminding us of simpler times, offers a much-needed sanctuary where we can be outside with all the comforts of home.

Enclosures at the Street Edge

When we erect a hedge, fence, or wall along the street edge, we are putting a kind of belt around our property, delineating what's private from what's public. Depending upon the degree of enclosure we prefer, this perimeter boundary can be more or less open for viewing by passersby. A low picket fence extends the architecture of the house to the street edge, keeping animals and children in and strangers out. Always consider the style of architecture in relationship to the choice of fence.

There are times when privacy needs dictate the use of a tall hedge, fence, or wall along the front of a property. For example, if you live in a high-traffic neighborhood,

TURNING THE CORNER

Don't forget that a fence is an enclosure: It should look as though it actually encloses something. Always turn the corner on a fence; otherwise, it looks as though the slightest breeze could push it over. If you're enclosing only a portion of your yard, then anchor the fence to the house in a way that relates harmoniously to its facade.

This Los Angeles house sits almost to the edge of its corner lot. Rather than erecting walls against the sidewalk, its innovative owner planted tall hedges and created a low-maintenance stone landscape in the median strip.

(above left) A deep bed along the street edge with easy-care plantings that span the seasons can be enjoyed by the owners and neighbors alike.

(above right) It's refreshing to find a new neighborhood community where the developer protected, rather than removed, the existing trees. Although grouped closely together, these homes feel as though they sit in a wilderness.

(facing page) It doesn't take much to form a sense of sanctuary, even on a small lot. This well-designed combination of gateway, fences, low walls, and plantings gives privacy to a suburban side yard.

THE NEIGHBORING ZONE

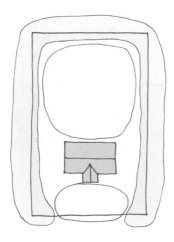

you may need an enclosure to bring a sense of security to your home. It helps to find ways to create a sense of neighborliness while still walling yourselves off by planting a garden on the median between sidewalk and street or creating a peek-a-boo gateway that allows visitors to look in even if they can't enter.

The Neighboring Zone

When you live in a community with others, having—and being—a good neighbor makes living there both comfortable and pleasurable. Neighbors can watch over your house while you're away, doing helpful things like bringing in the mail, watering your plants, or feeding the animals. Good neighbors will be there to help shovel snow or mow the lawn for the elderly. Neighborhood kids can ride bikes together, while adults enjoy block parties with their neighbors, cooking out, or having a long, cool drink on the front porch together.

But not all neighbors are good ones. Those who have messy yards, barking dogs, unruly kids, or unorthodox habits can wreak havoc on your daily life. To maintain your property as a comfort zone, you need to make sure the design of the Neighboring Zone is handled appropriately. This zone covers the perimeter of your property— the side and rear boundaries of your land (as well as the front). You can choose to open up or close off visual and physical access by the way you create "enclosing arms" around your home.

Enclosing Arms

Home is the place where you feel safe and find refuge. Like being hugged by a loved one, encircling your house so that it feels enclosed brings a comforting sense of security to your property. Enclosing arms—walls, fences, screens, and hedges—mark and guard the territory around your home against intrusion from outside, while offering sanctuary and seclusion within.

PRIVACY SCREENS

One of the first and most important tasks I often complete for my clients is the creation of a privacy barrier around their house. This might mean installing a fence or an evergreen screen that gives shelter, obliterates unsightly views, or blocks out noise from rambunctious neighbors. Sometimes this means filling in gaps.

Some recent clients of mine who moved to an in-town residential neighborhood renovated their house to take advantage of a neighboring 80-year-old beech tree and other plantings that separated them from their neighbor. Alas, the neighboring house was sold to a developer who renovated it into four large condominiums. Without getting town approval, he cut down the ancient beech tree, leaving my clients with a huge gaping hole at the edge of their property, fully exposed to the neighbors.

The condominiums sat at a higher elevation than the clients' house, so a fence would not begin to block out windows, headlights, and other distractions. Instead, the solution was to bring in several large trees to "plug the holes" and face them down with lower trees and shrubs so that this verdant enclosure looks as though it has always been there.

¹ The original view to the neighbor.

² Trees down, condos up.

³ Saved by the screen.

A landscape's enclosure can take many forms. A fence can define a yard, a hedge can mark a garden room, or a wall can surround a compound. Some enclosures are impenetrable, made of mud-and-wattle, concrete, brick, or stone. Others are screens that afford a filtered view to a distant landscape. And some enclosures act as backdrops to garden elements, while others are the elements themselves—such as a perennial border that is both a wall and a focal point within a garden space.

Enclosure Creates Expansion

If you live on a small property, you may be concerned that erecting an enclosure around its perimeter will make it feel even smaller. However, the opposite is in fact true: Enclosure creates expansion. Some years ago, I designed a condominium garden for a couple in a city on a tiny site bordered by a small urban forest in the rear and a neighbor's yard on either side. My clients wanted a serene outdoor haven—a bluestone terrace surrounded by woodland plantings within their 1,000-sq.-ft. space.

(left) You don't need a high, solid fence to create a feeling of privacy around your house. Here, a 5-ft.-tall fence is made of wide boards that are nailed to either side of a post in an alternating pattern—a horizontal version of a traditional "shadowbox" design.

(bottom left) A low, whitewashed brick wall encloses a garden courtyard, extending the presence of home by completing the architecture in the landscape.

(bottom right) Take away this high board fence and you'd no longer know whose property is whose. The fence is a clear boundary line, and it also creates the illusion of a foreground and a background.

After I ordered a 6-ft.-high board fence to define the site, I was a little worried that this enclosure would make the garden feel even smaller than it was. When I came back after the fence was installed, I was amazed to discover that the space seemed to have mysteriously grown overnight.

Why would enclosing an area make it feel more expansive? It's because every square inch of space within an enclosure becomes important, every corner is revealed, the middle becomes inhabitable, and the background stays respectfully behind the fence. Everything is in its place. And the garden itself feels, in my terms, sacred, set apart from the outside world as a special—and very secret—realm.

Layering plants against an enclosure can also make a space feel larger than it really is. Adding trees, shrubs, tall grasses, and perennials alongside a fence or wall tends to soften the effect of an enclosure by filling the edges with billows of color and texture that bring interest to a backyard landscape, engaging the eye and stimulating the senses.

(facing page) Soft arms of plantings intermingled with latticework walls make a cozy green room for eating outdoors.

(top left and bottom) Mary Dewart of Dewart Design subdivided a broad, bare backyard into a series of garden rooms, making the whole feel expansive and beautiful. The largest "room," pictured here, turns the space into a play lawn surrounded by wide planting beds filled with easy-care perennials such as black-eyed Susans, daisies, Red Hot Poker, and daylilies.

(top right) In the Southwest, "coyote" fencing made of juniper branches is stuck into the ground to keep critters out of pasturelands and gardens. This Santa Fe landscape is also contained by layers of dazzling plants set in retaining walls that step up the slope.

A ROOM WITHIN ROOMS

This tiny walled courtyard in the heart of the Capitol Hill district of Washington, D.C., measures only 22 ft. by 26 ft., but because it is subdivided into tiny rooms, it feels much more spacious. Landscape designer Maggie Judycki of GreenThemes, Inc., became involved in this project after the homeowner's architect, Jerald L. Clark, had already designed all of the brickwork. Every square inch has been masterfully crafted, juxtaposing a handsome outdoor brick gathering space with a hip-roofed storage shed and a contemplative sitting area sized just for two.

The owner, influenced by the great estates and gardens of Europe, wanted a space to entertain in and enjoy after work, as well as a garden for setting out his favorite plants. Maggie initially worked on the redesign and installation of a new cedar pergola over the small corner seating area. She then designed a limestone bas-relief to give a subtle focus to the little room and placed a backless limestone bench against one of the walls, much like examples the owner had seen in historic English gardens. Topped by the handsome pergola and vines, with "art" on the wall and a place to sit, the whole corner

turned into a separate room and a destination for the eye from inside the 1878 house.

With its basketweave paver pattern edged by planters set at sitting height, the whole space feels venerable yet fresh; cozy but roomy. Because it is built almost entirely of brick, it feels like a set of indoor rooms out of doors—the kind of retreat many city dwellers long for.

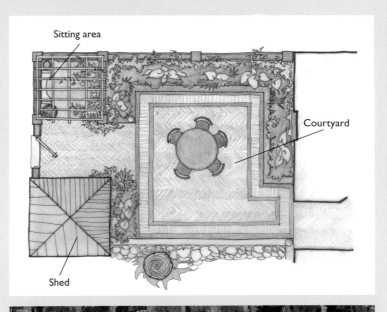

[1] The fine details in the small brick courtyard tie the design together: the border around the "rug" of brick underfoot, the repeating archways with black trim, and the variety of foliage plantings.

[2] Brick, limestone, and wood combine to make a charming room within a room for an intimate twosome.

[3] The carved limestone bas-relief provides a formal focal element that echoes the material of the bench and blends perfectly with the mortared joints of the brick wall.

We can subdivide our enclosures to make them feel even more expansive than the space created by just four walls. Imagine wandering through my clients' little condo garden if it were further subdivided into two rooms. Defined by clear edges, the garden would appear to have eight separate walls, eight distinct corners, and two central open spaces, and each garden could feel completely different from the other. One could be filled with symmetrical formal plantings, a fountain, and a bench; the other with a terrace, table and chairs, and a view to the neighboring woods. Simply by subdividing and enclosing a space, your landscape will seem bigger, more diverse, and enticingly mysterious. When you are unable to grasp the whole with one glance, your property becomes a broader realm to explore.

The architecture of the house has been pushed out to the edge of the street, marking the entrance to this property. These stuccoed concrete walls are built to look like traditional adobe.

Enclosing with Walls

When security is an issue, you may choose to build a thick concrete or stucco wall to keep noises and intruders at bay. Think of a wall as being part of the architecture of your house, like partitions that have been pushed out to the property line. Match details such as type of siding, stain or paint color, and choice of trim. If you're attaching any part of an enclosure to the house, look for opportunities that will make the connection feel seamless.

Perimeter walls that encircle a house can take many forms. As discussed on p. 26, if you live on top of or below a slope, making retaining walls that hold back the earth allows you to support vertical grade changes for terracing or level areas of play. Low walls can also surround a property, especially when combined with fencing or hedging to create a more permeable screen between inside and out.

(left) A handsome openwork fence sits on pieced walls between thick stone piers. The rails of the fence and gate line up perfectly, a pleasing detail that brings coherence to the whole.

(bottom left) Plants cascade over a retaining wall of dry stacked stones. A tiny path light illuminates the steps.

(bottom right) Retaining walls help level out a sloping property to create terraces that can be used for gardens, strolling, or play.

RELATE THE FENCE TO THE HOUSE

A scalloped picket fence brings a touch of adornment to this simple country home.

The unadorned facade of this Georgian-style house is a good backdrop for a more ornate openwork fence.

When you live really close to your neighbors, you can use fencing both to achieve privacy and to encourage friendliness. Build a board fence just high enough to block views when seated and an openwork "topper" so you can say hello over the fence.

DID YOU KNOW?

In many communities, codes require that you place the rail side of the fence facing your side, not the neighbors'. Be sure to check with your local building inspector to determine the code regarding fence heights, locations, and styles for your particular municipality.

(far left) Salvaged boards of varying heights and widths are spaced an inch apart along fence rail of different species. This allows for good air flow while still providing privacy.

(left) Don't be afraid to make it personal. The "hand" picket tells you just where to pull open the gate.

Enclosing with Fences

"Good fences make good neighbors," or so the saying goes. I think it's true, for more than the obvious reasons. Yes, a fence can help to mark off your property line, so there's no confusion about who owns what. And, as it has done throughout history, a perimeter barrier keeps children and animals in and unwanted critters out. Done right, an enclosure around your property can serve to embrace it as your habitat of home—the place you feel most comfortable in the world. Good fences can make your backyard a sanctuary of beauty and meaning—a personal piece of paradise that you've carved out as your own. Here are some tips for making good fences.

Let the house be your guide to style and color A fence is really an extension of your house into the landscape. To bring a sense of harmony between inside and out to your property, look for ways to relate the layout and details of your fence to the architecture of your home.

Match the style of fence to the house. For example, a cape or a colonial house is nicely set off by a picket or a simple board fence; a low-slung contemporary looks good with a horizontal railing made of unadorned wood or steel cable. A gracious Greek Revival looks wonderful with formal columns and spindles; a brightly painted bungalow can stand up to a variety of fence styles, including latticework, slatted, or even one of your own design.

Design with proportion in mind When laying out a fence, use the facade of your house as a means to create harmony between house and garden. If possible, choose the spacing of the posts to relate to the window or column spacing of your house. Also, if the fence sits close to the house, select a height that connects to some aspect of the facade: the windowsill height or the front porch railing height, for instance.

Try to place a path or a fence opening so that at least part of it aligns with a door or window. This doesn't necessarily mean that you have to create a walkway directly on axis; a meandering walkway works as well.

LINE IT UP

Orient your fence with an architectural detail. Here, the top of the fence lines up with the window mullion.

GOOD FENCES, GOOD NEIGHBORS

If you live close to your neighbors, a good fence can feel like a security blanket around your entire property. But if you are uncomfortable walling yourself off completely, the fences shown here suggest a variety of ways to allow partial views in.

1. A low rail fence delineates the property line and marks what's private from what's public.

2. An openwork topper.

3. Fences can be playful, too, just like their owners.

4. A lattice fence is an excellent support for vines.

5. Living branches can be woven together to create an enclosure.

6. Lattice fencing defines a garden room.

7. A fence can become a personal work of landscape art. This one is of galvanized steel with "vines" twining their way through it.

8. A woven wattle fence brings a natural feel to a shady corner.

CONSIDER THE SLOPE OF YOUR SITE

Choosing where to site your fence on your property can be tricky. Fences usually look best when set on level ground, but most properties have elevation changes that need to be considered.

There are two ways to deal with a fence on a sloping site. One is to "rake" the fence, cutting the bottom of the boards on an angle to follow the topography. This is typically done with an informal, rustic fence like a stockade fence that often is erected far from the house. Another is to step the fence. This is usually done with a more formal fence that has a top and bottom cap and frame. It's preferable to create regular intervals that the steps conform to: For example, every 8 ft., the fence steps down 12 in. This gives a consistent, rhythmic pattern that feels intentional, which is always a good quality in design.

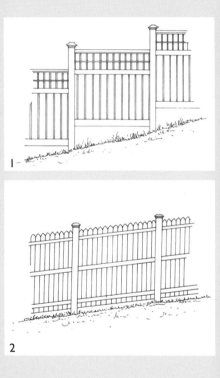

¹ This board fence with topper steps down the slope in increments along both its top and bottom.

² You can "rake" a stockade type fence by following the slope.

³ Fences that are more architectural (with squared-off posts, rails, and a cap on top, for example) look best on slopes if they move up or down in sections with regular steps, using the same height up or down.

Finding privacy while inviting your neighbors in Homeowners who live in close-knit neighborhoods often seek seclusion in their backyard but don't feel right completely walling off their neighbors. Both situations might benefit from a concept I call "open enclosures," where family privacy can coexist with neighborly contact. Screens, privacy fences, and hedges can all be used.

Openwork fencing such as latticework panels, picket fencing, cabling, or wire fencing allows air, light, and communication between properties. A combination of lattice panels and trees and shrubs lets you share your garden with passersby while still feeling private within.

Some of us live in communities where privacy is at a premium. Townhouse or cottage community dwellers with only a small piece of ground usually look for ways to ensure that their precious land feels private and not open to scrutiny or intrusion by others. Often, stringent condominium association guidelines allow only certain fence and gate styles and heights in order to control the look of the entire community. Sometimes you can use plantings to layer in privacy, but here, too, there may be strict height restrictions and a limited plant list to choose from.

An apartment dweller lucky enough to have a deck still seeks privacy. Lattice panels screwed to planters encourage air flow into a sunny space, give a structure for vines and tall perennials, and screen out the neighbors.

PUBLIC TO PRIVATE

When you live in a close-knit community, creating a sense of privacy between you, your neighbors, the commons area, and the street is crucial to your sense of well-being. In this charming neighborhood of 16 cottages on the outskirts of Seattle, Washington, the feeling of seclusion is created by careful layering from the most public zone to the most private, with fencing, plantings, and the utmost care given to the delineation of exterior and interior spaces.

Architect Ross Chapin has crafted each unit with meticulous detailing, open floor plans, and sizeable porches that are oriented around a common green where gathering is encouraged and movies are shown on hot summer nights. The cottages also share a community center known as the Club, a tool shed, and communal garbage enclosures located near the groups of garages at the rear of the property. The public spaces are beautifully planted by Seattle gardener Todd Paul, with drifts of perennials at the base of the massive conifers that have been carefully preserved to give overhead shelter to the new community.

Each unit enjoys a spacious front porch and a small backyard, enclosed by simple wooden fencing whose boards are set with spacing between them to let in light and air. Along the street, an edge of grass separates the sidewalk from a front garden of grasses, daylilies, and herbs. These are divided by a low split-rail fence that marks the property line of each home. Behind the fence is each unit's private garden space, set below the front porches. The same colorful layering effect happens along the common green and community center, lending an exuberant atmosphere to the whole neighborhood.

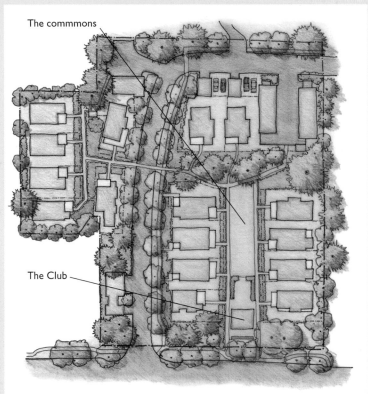

The commmons

The Club

[1] Eight of the houses in the "pocket neighborhood" are oriented around a public commons. The 1,600-sq.-ft. single-family dwellings measure roughly half the size of most new homes today.

[2] The community is laid out around groupings of mature trees, in an attempt to balance development pressures with the legacy of the land.

[3] The Club is the central gathering place for the residents of the community.

¹ In a narrow band of only 15 ft., a series of layers moves from most public to most private: from the green, to the sidewalk, to a common planting strip, to a fence that marks the property line, and then to layers of plantings or lawn, to the front porch. The layers continue inside to the living room, to the den, and finally out back to the private garden.

² Each house is designed so that the "active" parts lie near the public realm—the living room faces the green or the common walkway, for instance, so you can tell who's coming and who's going. These eyes on the street are particularly helpful for those who are living alone, are infirm or elderly, or have small children.

³ Communal tool sheds and garbage corrals are the kinds of places where people get to know each other in the course of daily life; they're where a caring neighbor can become a caring friend.

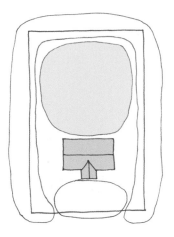

The Living Zone

Clearly one of the most important comfort zones on your property is the house itself. Its sheltering roof and protective walls provide a safe harbor from the outside world. Whether you occupy a townhouse, a log cabin, or a raised ranch, your dwelling is the place where you *live,* with spaces for gathering and for getting away, as well as areas for working, playing, cooking, bathing, and sleeping.

The same activities that happen inside a house can also happen outside. Outdoor kitchens, showers, and living spaces are amenities that are increasingly popular these days. To understand how to plan the amenities around the outside of your house, it's important to understand how the inside relates to the outside. What works best next to what? In this section, we look at each of the living zones and how they relate to the home outside.

(top right) We're all drawn to sunlight and to views. When you locate your outdoor dining area in the place that makes the most of these features, you'll use it all the time.

(bottom right) Although this is a large house, it sits on a piece of land that can support its size. One improvement would be to install a large tree, which would bring shade in the heat of summer and reduce the relative scale of the house.

This little dooryard garden is well proportioned to this cape-style home. When you add the facade plus the roofline height, the total height approximates the depth of this low-walled enclosure.

HOW BIG IS THE YARD?

If possible, the width of green space in front of a house should be at least equal to the height of a house's front facade.

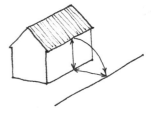

Fitting the House to the Land

How much living space do you really need? What is left over after you fit your house onto your land? Some sites are just too small for their houses. Or more accurately, some houses are just too big for their sites. With the recent spate of teardowns in suburbs around the country, too-large homes are replacing smaller-scale bungalows, capes, and cottages. When an oversize structure alters the scale, rhythm, style, and character of a neighborhood, it also changes our perception of the front, side, and back yards, since the house occupies so much more of the land area of the parcel than do the other homes around it. Suddenly, a house seems to loom over its setting, rather than "sitting pretty" with the right amount of breathing room around it.

Just what is the right amount of space around a house? It depends on the context. A four-story townhouse on Commonwealth Avenue in Boston that has a tiny front yard looks just right because it enjoys a wide sidewalk in front and a handsome park that runs down the middle of the divided avenue. When you add the private to the public green space, the total amount seems appropriate in relation to the height of the house. A one-story bungalow in Austin, Texas, looks great on a tiny property or a large one. But the rule of thumb for front yards is that the ideal green space in front of a house should be at least equal to the height of a house's front facade.

Hearth and Helm

In earlier times, the center of a house was always wherever the hearth was—the place around which the family sat, got warm, conversed, baked, and cooked. Today, the kitchen incorporates the activities of the traditional hearth and has become the center of the contemporary home, the radiating core from which a host of other activities emanate. Perhaps a better term for today's kitchen is the helm—the position of control where the different activities come together. I'm sure you weren't expecting a

DID YOU KNOW?

The overall relationship between the size of your house and the size of your property can be quantified according to its floor area ratio (FAR). This is the ratio of the total building square footage divided by its site square footage. Anti-teardown zoning ordinances often use FARs to limit the size of buildings on small lots.

Good views from the kitchen connect inside to out. A dining deck sits just outside the kitchen, allowing for easy access with trays of food when entertaining.

discussion of kitchens in a landscape design book. But how you live your life inside your house is closely related with the way you live outside—home doesn't stop at the walls of the house.

Inside the house, just off the kitchen, you'll normally find a dining area, a mudroom, and a family and/or living room—the main living areas. In the typical new home, these areas are open to each other, marked off by different window types, ceiling heights, paint colors, or flooring choices. Windows in the kitchen commonly offer views out onto the front or back yards, extending the sense of visual access out onto the landscape.

Outside the house, just off the kitchen, you'll likely find an outdoor eating area in the form of a screened porch, a deck, or a patio. Such proximity is important. Chances are you won't eat outside if you have to carry trays of food a long distance

DINING IN, DINING OUT

The author's kitchen sits at the corner of the house between similarly sized indoor and outdoor dining spaces and right next to a screened porch (the summer living room). Note the varying size of the deck, narrowest at the dining room where views out when seated are most important and widest where outdoor eating takes place.

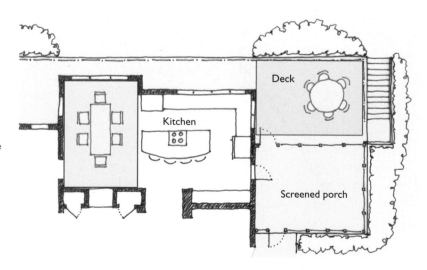

from the kitchen. Climbing more than two or three stairs while carrying trays is difficult work, so keeping an outdoor eating area on the same level as the kitchen will ensure that it gets well used.

A well-designed kitchen should also have a direct view out to the backyard and the different activities that go on there. Yet many homes today are built into the side of a hill, with a playroom below and living area above. This creates the problem of a high deck that sits a full story above the ground. The deck fulfills the requirements of being just off the kitchen and offers easy access for outdoor dining and entertaining, but it sits so high up that access to the backyard is difficult at best. Visual access down to the backyard is often blocked by the decking itself, so it's hard to see what's going on down below. One possible solution is to make the stairs down to the yard into a series of short runs of steps with generous landings at rhythmic intervals. Where there are landings, you can add a bench or perch—a great place to look out from and talk with people as you make your way down to ground level.

Outdoor kitchens don't have to be elaborate. A portable gas barbecue sits under its own enclosure in this small Canadian garden. Make sure to bring comfortable chairs alongside so your friends can talk to you as you grill.

Another way to reconfigure a high deck is as a series of small outdoor platforms that tier down in steps to the backyard below. At the top might be a grilling and dining area, just off the kitchen. The next level could be an outdoor living area that sits above the backyard. The lowest level could incorporate a hot tub, tool shed, or storage space, or become a small gathering space for an intimate twosome.

What other outdoor activities need to be near the helm of your house? Unless you have an elaborate outdoor kitchen complete with grill, sink, and refrigerator installed somewhere in your backyard, you'll need to keep outdoor cooking equipment such as a charcoal or gas grill or smoker close to your indoor kitchen. Having piping-hot grilled meat or vegetables at the ready adds to the pleasure of alfresco dining. It also helps to locate a back entranceway and/or mudroom close to the kitchen so that you don't have to haul groceries a long distance.

If an area close to your kitchen enjoys six hours or more of full sun, you can locate small herb, vegetable, or cutting gardens nearby. It's wonderful to be able to nip

(above) The high deck works because its underside is covered by lattice. A 10-ft.-tall rhododendron masks much of its height, and a stairway leads down to the play spaces below.

(left) A compost bin for kitchen scraps and garden clippings just beneath your kitchen window makes wonderful use of a narrow side yard.

(facing page) This deck seems to float above the garden space below. While the decking follows the line of the house, the curving rail works well with the landscape forms around it.

A MODEST MAKEOVER

Sometimes a landscape makeover entails just a few deft moves. The owner of this San Francisco property wanted a private outdoor sitting area between her house and garage. Landscape designer Alma Hecht decided to tear out the existing rotten wood deck that sat just behind the garage, thereby reconnecting her client to the ground.

Alma created a patio of mica-flecked gray canyon flagstones and recycled concrete pieces, visually united by native burgundy ground cover. Then she painted the blank wall of the garage a rich amber color to create a complementary backdrop for an espaliered California flannelbush and terra-cotta pots of flowering plants. The resulting outdoor gathering space is both intimate enough for one yet expansive enough for celebrations with friends.

Replacing the deck with a patio, sprucing up the wall color, and planting an espaliered tree completely transformed this backyard gathering place.

out and clip fresh basil for *caprese* salads, oregano for pizzas, mint for iced tea, or nasturtiums as an edible garnish. If you have no sunny ground nearby, then plant herbs in flower boxes that hang off the kitchen windows or place large containers on your deck to keep your favorite cooking flavors close at hand. And don't forget to plan for a compost area just off the kitchen, which will help turn vegetable scraps into valuable fertilizer for your garden.

The Gathering Zone

Gathering zones around your property include transitional areas that hug the house and intersect with the landscape such as decks, screened porches, terraces, and patios. Another gathering zone, the play zone, might be a section of level ground where outdoor play can take place, including areas for children's play structures, family games like croquet and badminton, or swimming pools and their related outbuildings.

Outdoor living spaces also benefit from having a "ceiling" to filter light and control sunlight. This steel and wood trellis structure works as a space definer as well.

While each of these gathering zones houses a collective function where many may congregate, getaway zones are outdoor "away rooms" for more private, intimate, or relaxing pursuits. You can locate either gathering or getaway spaces so that they enjoy different vantages from or onto the property.

You might also choose to locate and design your gathering and getaway zones so that they occupy your preferred vantage points. Look back to "Places to Be" on p. 45 to remember the places that came to mind as you read through this material. For many of us, our living spaces should feel cozy and intimate. For others, occupying the center makes us feel good. Some of us prefer to sit high up; others like nestling into a deep and dark place. Knowing which of these places we prefer to be helps us create the outdoor world that works best for ourselves and our loved ones.

Transition areas Transition areas lie between the inside and outside of the house. Typically a porch, deck, terrace, or balcony, a transition area gives us a place to take

This is not so much a deck as a platform that hangs out over the edge of a retaining wall at the edge of the property. A high railing (40 in. by code) serves both to protect viewers from falling off the end and as a back to the dining table and chairs that perch there.

a breather—to notice the view, check out the day's weather, extend the entertaining space, or have a side conversation in the middle of a party. For some, it's a space just outside the house where you can have a quiet cup of coffee or enjoy an evening cocktail. For others, it might be a balcony where you can slip away outside to play a guitar.

Porches As discussed earlier in this chapter, a porch is a transitional space for gathering or getting away that nestles below a protective roof, adjacent to the house. Porches can be located on any floor of the house, in the front, side, or back, and may be open on three sides or screened to ward off marauding insects. (It helps to screen under your decking, too, so that mosquitoes don't find their way in between the slats.)

Decks As wooden platforms that sit above ground, decks are usually extensions of the living area outside the walls of the house. They may be open to the sky or topped by wooden or steel shade structures on which vines can be grown for flowers, scent,

(left) People are drawn to areas inside and outside their houses that are either sunken or raised in relation to the rest of their home. This little getaway zone sits up a few steps from the play space, tucked in against a privacy hedge and overtopped with an umbrella-like canopy.

(bottom left) Believe it or not, this cheery gathering space sits right next to a utility yard, located just behind the old painted louvered doors. It doesn't take much to freshen up a dark area like this: brightly patterned pillows, potted plants, and some fresh paint applied to a couple of well-worn chairs.

(bottom right) Decks can be squeezed into the tightest of corners. Market umbrellas of many sizes, colors, and materials offer the possibility of portable shade.

SELECT MATERIALS RESPONSIBLY

Your choice of building materials can have a significant environmental impact. Many homeowners are choosing new recycled decking (and fencing) materials to minimize upkeep. One problem is that recycled decking is difficult to renew or repair once scuffed or stained because it can't be sanded. An alternative is to use sustainably grown hardwoods such as mahogany and ipe.

or visual interest. Decks can be cantilevered—supported at only one end—or held off the ground with columns or posts.

As an extension of the architecture of the house, a deck should look and feel as though it is integral to the design of the whole, not an appendage. As discussed earlier, many decks sit a full story above the backyard play space they're meant to relate to, creating an awkward or unsightly space below its floor and difficulty in getting down from on high. Other decks are too narrow to be useful. A comfortable dimension for a table and chairs is at least 10 ft. around. Some decks are so huge that they overwhelm the outdoor furniture placed there, as well as the house itself.

Decks also benefit from shade structures overhead, such as pergolas, trellises, or retractable awnings. Market umbrellas are another good way to create shade, especially around an outdoor dining table. If you design your deck around a single-stemmed tree, it not only provides shade but also breaks up the expanse of the deck and provides a visual point of focus.

Your choice of deck railings is important to the look and feel of your platform in the sky. Check your local building code for the regulations about railing heights and spacing. Most townships mandate a railing height from 34 in. to 38 in., with 6-in. spacing between the balusters so that infants and children cannot fall through. Thus, many railings are composed of vertical wooden balusters set closely together, much like a banister on a staircase. The only problem with this solution is that the

In a close-knit neighborhood, a deck can feel exposed. Here, the closely spaced pickets provide a degree of privacy without blocking the view of the landscape.

rails tend to block out the view below. Other possible railing details include ornamental fretwork—intricate patterns of wooden cutouts, metal or steel rails, or cable railings that are stretched thin between railings (as shown in the top right photo on p. 131). If you think of your deck as a piece of furniture that is visually related to the architectural details of the house, you will create a transitional space that links inside to outside in an elegant way.

Stone underfoot A terrace is another space that's made for gathering outdoors. A paved or grassy area commonly installed just outside a house, a patio can be used for dining alfresco, sitting under the stars, or entertaining around a swimming pool, hot tub, outdoor fireplace, or fire pit. Paving allows homeowners to create outdoor rooms, terraces, and patios. Some homeowners pave over most of their yard with stamped concrete or other impervious materials in an effort to cut down on maintenance. If you opt for this route, leave cracks or planting pockets, or consider using gravel as the terrace surface: Adding plant material to hardscaping not only reduces runoff and absorbs heat but also provides a habitat for wildlife.

Different shapes, sizes, and materials can be turned into just the right type of terrace for the kind of outdoor living you want to do. Bluestone, limestone, fieldstone, and concrete pavers can all be used in a variety of ways to extend the presence of home into the landscape. All look best when softened with plantings at their edges.

(below left) Cut stones sunken in grass limit wear and tear to the lawn. A rectangular stone terrace under the seating area ensures dry feet and a stable surface for dining under the stars.

(below right) Using gravel or peastone underfoot reduces costs, provides excellent drainage, and requires only an occasional raking to look its best. Be sure to edge it well; otherwise it will migrate onto nearby lawns or be carried on shoes inside the house.

CREATE A SUSTAINABLE LAWN

Use native grasses such as buffalo grass rather than a conventional lawn seed mix to create a sustainable lawn. Buffalo grass is cold hardy, drought tolerant, and thrives from Arizona to the Dakotas. It will grow into a dense, green lawn that needs minimal water and little or no mowing.

The Play Zone

Inside the house, our basements are often play zones for our families, where we watch television, play ping-pong or pool, or keep exercise equipment. Similarly, creating a level play space just outside the house allows free flow between inside and out and space for games, parties, and outdoor entertainment.

If you have a big enough yard, creating a level area of about 30 ft. by 60 ft. will give you enough room to play a host of games, including badminton, bocce, and croquet. Make sure you've seeded in short grass and that the play area slopes slightly away from the house for good drainage. If you live up on a hill, create a low parapet wall that's at sitting height (from 15 in. to 18 in. high) to catch errant soccer balls before they roll down the hill. Keeping a level paved surface as part of your driveway allows you and your family to shoot hoops, play four-square, hopscotch, or even an old-fashioned game of jacks.

(right) Children enjoy wooden play sets but also need to explore nature. The clearing at the back of this property allows for both structured and natural play, all within view of the house.

(below) Bocce is a fun—and competitive—outdoor sport that can be played by two or four people on a gravel court or a long, narrow lawn area.

If you're thinking about creating a family swimming pool, the first thing to consider is safety. Make sure you design it so that a retractable, lockable pool cover may be used when the pool is not in use, typically as a long rectangle. Install a pool enclosure around the perimeter of your pool. Most building codes specify a 5-ft.-high nonclimbable fence with a self-locking gate.

Pools these days are normally constructed of gunite, a concrete material that is sprayed from a high-pressure gun onto a structure of reinforced steel rods or mesh. The concrete can be tinted to a dark color to give the effect of endless depth, or aggregate can be added to create different textures and colors both within the pool and around it. Other choices for the pool deck—the terrace that surrounds the pool—include the same wide range of materials as for entertainment terraces (such as limestone, granite, or even wood decking).

The Getaway Zone

Inside your house, you seek out getaway zones when you want some privacy, as places away from the hustle and bustle of family life. Your bedroom is one such getaway zone, as is your study, library, or attic.

Just as the getaway zone inside your house is on high, down deep, or at the very edge, so too the outside getaway zone is usually located at a remote part of your site. What kinds of activities would you prefer to do in private on your land? Napping in a hammock? Sleeping under the stars? Trysting within an arbor? Reading while propped against a mossy mound? Such outdoor away rooms draw us to the edge where we can get away while still being within reach of the house.

Diagramming the spaces we occupy every day using the different comfort zones—Surrounding, Welcoming, Neighboring, and Living—helps us determine what can happen in the various areas around our house. The next step is to figure out how to link these areas together by creating a system of paths and places that flow harmoniously throughout the property.

(above left) Children enjoy wooden play sets but also need to explore nature. The clearing at the back of this property allows for both structured and natural play, all within view of the house.

(above right) Kitty-corner benches sit beneath an ironwork pergola. In small properties, getaway and gathering zones sometimes combine into one.

Many of us prefer to locate our getaway zones in the most remote point on our property. The huge tree marks the corner of this lakeside yard where a table and chairs perch beneath it at the very edge.

Making It Flow

I t's wonderful to live on a property with a landscape that flows. As you walk around your yard, each space seems to unfold effortlessly into the next. Just as inside your house a well-designed hallway leads you to different living spaces, so too an exterior path moves you from one area to another—whether its basic layout is Immersed or Exposed, Central Clearing, House Front and Center, Open-Air Rooms, or a hybrid of all four. Your property's aesthetic arrangement—All Lined Up, On the Angle, or Voluptuous Curves—also influences the way you move through your property. To make it flow, there are a few easy-to-apply ideas that can transform an everyday landscape into a satisfying journey through your home outside.

So what do we mean by "flow"? Flow happens when something moves freely from one place to another in an unbroken stream. It is important in design because creating a sense of flow links different Comfort Zones to one another, such as the front yard to the back, the inside of the house to the outside, and a view of something to its vantage point.

"A fine landscape is like a piece of music; it must be taken at the right tempo."
—PAUL SCOTT MOWRER, *The House of Europe*

Creating a landscape that flows may sound like a difficult task, but it's not. There are really only three kinds of flow in a landscape: *moving*—the flow created by "paths to follow"; *pausing*—the temporary break in the flow at "places to pause"; and *stopping*—a halt in the flow in order to enjoy "spaces to sit." When you put all these activities together, you can choreograph movement through your property so that it flows.

Paths to Follow

No matter its size, every property offers opportunities to create paths to follow. Front and back walks, stepping-stone paths, grassy ways, trails through the woods, and even your driveway all benefit from a thoughtful, flowing design. A good path to follow is hard to resist as it takes us on a physical journey through space by linking one experience on your property to another.

If you live in a northern clime, the best time to study the flow of your property is in winter when the bones of the land are evident—especially after a snowfall.

What are the kinds of experiences you'd like to connect? There's the sidewalk to the front door, the front walk to the side of the house, and the side of the house to the backyard. You can also link the deck to the terrace, and the terrace to the hammock, fire pit, playhouse, or other special feature on your property. If you have the space, you might even want to create paths through a grove, to a high point, or through a garden. Even in the smallest of landscapes, you can make a path of just a few stepping stones that passes by a modest bench along the way.

Getting Started: Mapping the Journey

A path is really just a journey that takes you from point A to point B. Along the way, you may pause to enjoy special features, take in a scene or view, and then move on until you finally reach a stopping place—your destination. When you think of a path as a journey, it's not hard to lay out the route you'd like it to take around your property.

(above left) Like a beautiful piece of music with no jarring notes, your property seems to "sing" when its elements flow. Without flow, a property is made up of a series of unrelated spaces and objects; with flow, these spaces and objects are placed in such a way that they relate harmoniously.

(above center) The experience of "flow" can also happen in a more modest setting. Here, the rhythm of the stepping stones stands out amongst the plantings all around.

(above right) The S-curve formed by the line of the stepping stones is a wonderful path to follow, drawing you forward to a rustic sitting area that overlooks a wide, wide view.

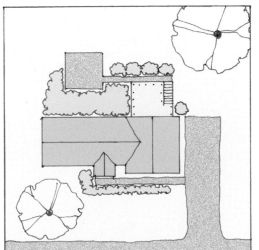
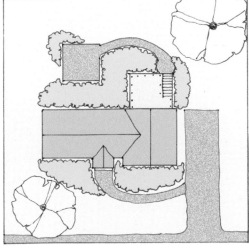

GOOD FLOW, BAD FLOW

In the example on the far left, straight paths hug the house and deck too closely, making a rigid, tight transition from place to place.

It is more comfortable to get from one location to another by way of curved paths that give some breathing room around structures, as shown in the drawing at left.

One way to map out your paths is to picture how water would flow around your property. Think of a straight walk as a man-made canal, a curving path as a meander in a stream, steps or staircases as a waterfall, and a patio or terrace as a pool or pond. Together these form a kind of river system that takes you on a journey around your landscape. People tend to move through space in much the same way water flows through a stream. They prefer to follow a "desire line"—the shortest route between one place and another, often the well-worn tracks between sidewalks. Observing or mapping the desire lines that you or your visitors naturally follow to enter, exit, and move around your property is a way to get started in designing your paths.

Special Features along the Way

Sometimes you may choose to lead yourself (or your visitor) from point A to point B in a more leisurely fashion, by stretching out the journey. The drawing on the facing page shows three different paths. One path leads directly from the house to a getaway

(above) This man-made waterfall looks much like one in nature, falling in a series of steps and widening out as a pool at the bottom.

(right) Like a waterfall, this outdoor staircase meanders down a hillside before opening out to a terrace—a pool of space.

(facing page) A narrow side path winds through a mossy shade garden, with its larger stones standing out and leading the way.

spot in a typical backyard. Contrast this with the longer, curving path that draws out the journey, taking you past a series of features along the way. Your path might first lead to a shady corner of the landscape where you walk into a small wood and then out again. It may then flow past a bright perennial border at the edge of the yard before landing at a sitting spot underneath a tree. These small but special focal areas are all short stopovers on the journey that you design to take people through your landscape. After all, a good landscape offers a chance for a leisurely stroll, rather than the usual headlong rush that constitutes the way most of us move through space.

Another way to lay out your path system is to map out each feature and draw in the connecting route. The third path in the drawing shows a short route but one that zigs and zags rather than heads straight for its destination. The walk time is longer, and its constantly changing direction encourages views to different parts of the landscape. The pacing and direction of your path give viewers powerful signals about where to go and even suggests how they might feel as they move through the space.

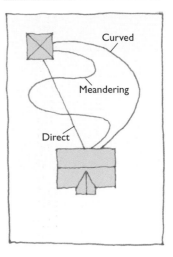

THREE TYPES OF PATH

Curved

Meandering

Direct

DID YOU KNOW?

Campus planners often install the main paths on the campus and then watch to see how students cut between them in order to pave the desire lines. You can do the same on your own property.

A POCKET-SIZE PATH IN D.C.

It's amazing what you can fit into a 20-ft. by 30-ft. space. This tiny backyard landscape, located in the heart of residential Washington, D.C., not far from the National Cathedral, sits sandwiched between other narrow row houses of its kind. Accessed by a back alley, a rear parking court is screened by a handsome openwork fence. Unattractive timber walls originally retained a 6-ft. grade change between the parking area at the top and the door to the rear of the house. A tiny patio sat crowded at the base of the house. A study in flow it was not.

Landscape designer Anya Zmudzka Sattler conceived of a completely new design for the space, based on a watery journey that curves its way down through stone "cheek" walls (the walls that are adjacent to the stairwell) to arrive at a circular terrace—the destination point. Anya used a variety of paving materials and extruded stones in the handsome water feature that forms the fulcrum of the garden. Making an asset out of the uphill sloping tiny backyard took some ingenuity, but the owners now reap the rewards when they relax outdoors in their oasis in the city.

The designer replaced the existing wooden retaining walls with an attractive stone wall and bluestone-treaded steps that wind their way down to a round seating area.

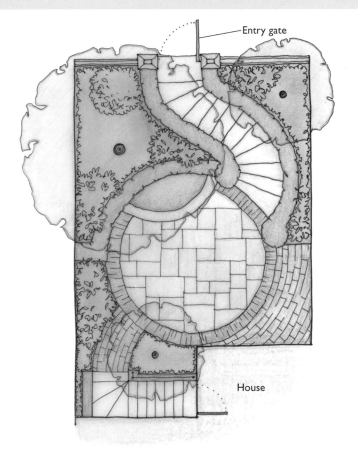

Entry gate

House

[1] The terrace is highlighted by a ring of brick around its border. The contrast in materials accentuates the circle of the terrace and echoes the rounded form of the stone piers.

[2] The wide bluestone cap around the water garden is built at sitting height—about 15 in. above the terrace floor.

[3] Nuzzled up to its neighbor, this narrow house and yard pack a lot of activities into one small space.

HIDE AND REVEAL

A useful design idea for creating interesting paths is to anticipate what views, scenes, or objects you'd like to *hide* along the way and what you'd like to *reveal,* then design the route of the path accordingly. For instance, you may want to skirt a view of your neighbor's garage by curving your path to avoid it, while exposing a gnarly old crabapple tree by sweeping the path right by its canopy.

Another way to hide and reveal is to use enclosures to obstruct a view and openings in those enclosures to frame one. I cover this idea in more detail in the section about framing on p. 192.

A salmon-colored wall comes as a surprise along this landscaped journey. The porthole-shaped openings invite travelers along the path to see what lies beyond.

(right) Two paths make it clear which way a newcomer is supposed to walk (along the solid, curving path) and which way a garden friend might choose (up the stepping-stone path).

(facing page) The natural stepping stones segue with ease into the cut-stone terrace with its cutouts for plantings.

Kinds of Paths

A path in the landscape can be made of one or more materials and a variety of surface textures (rough or smooth). It can be of different lengths and widths and follow a straight or meandering direction. Depending on your choice, you'll either move along a path looking straight ahead toward your destination or walk with downcast eyes, watching where you put your feet. Wider, smoother, and straighter paths tend to favor ease of movement; narrower, rougher, and meandering paths like those composed of stepping stones tend to force your gaze downward. For those of us who live in cold climates, choosing the right surface texture for a highly used path becomes critical when the snow flies. Make sure it passes the "shovel test" and is installed as a continuous level surface uninterrupted by cracks, juts, or bumps.

Choosing the Right Path

Visitors to a house often face a choice of paths: Should they use the walk to the front door or the one to the back? You can help them choose by the way you design the walkways. In general, straight, direct paths suggest purposeful striding toward a more public entryway, while curvilinear, meandering paths delineate a more informal entry to a private realm. A first-time visitor inevitably chooses a more formal, wide, long, and straight path that leads directly to the front door. A close friend or neighbor may take the shorter, informal stepping-stone path from driveway to back door.

When you consider the different functions a path can have, it's easy to imagine its size, shape, direction, and details. For instance, I think of the most private, least detectable type of path as a trail and a more public, wide, and easy-to-maneuver route as a promenade. In between is a walkway for two people side by side. In planning your landscape, you can use these distinctions to figure out where people should go, how they should travel, and what the path should look like underfoot.

PUT A STONE
UNDER YOUR STEP

Maybe it's the child in me, but I love to walk along a stepping-stone path. It reminds me of playing hopscotch as a girl, when I'd throw a stone into a chalked square and then hop, skip, or jump on the pavers, careful never to step on the lines. Strolling on stepping stones, I tread from stone to stone, eyes cast down, taking care not to step off into the mulch, ground cover, or lawn that surrounds them.

Stepping-stone paths are ideal for linking different parts of your garden. They can meander gracefully through a woodland landscape or march in strict geometric progression to form the front walk to your home. Regardless of how the stones are laid out, they instill a sense of continuous rhythm that entices us to follow them wherever they go. They also offer the practical benefits of being inexpensive and easy to install.

A hopscotch court is embedded as a permanent feature in this gravel walkway. One can only wonder what game the balls are for.

Stepping-Stone Paths

There's an almost infinite number of ways to run stepping-stone pathways, with far more options than simply installing evenly sized and spaced flagstones that march in a straight line across your yard. Here are some guidelines for placing stepping stones.

- **Vary the sizes of stones to define key points along a pathway.** Begin and end a landscaped journey with stones that are larger or more geometric than ones used for the rest of the path. The larger stones should be wide enough for someone to stand on with both feet. The size of stepping stones also serves as an indicator of where your eye should go. Small stones require you to look down as you place your feet. Larger stones allow you to plant both feet and look up to see what's around you. Wherever there is an "event" along a path, such as a view or a garden sculpture, place a larger stone so that a visitor can pause, look up, and notice the special scene.

- **Choose stones to create a mood that suits the setting.** Select smaller, natural fieldstone for a woodsy, contemplative stroll. Use larger, cut stones for a more formal or utilitarian pathway such as a front walk or a path linking a garage to house.

Cut stones set low in the ground for easy mowing seem to wander at will across a lawn panel.

(above left) Natural fieldstones lead through a blanket of spring-blooming woodland plantings beneath a canopy of stately spruces.

(above right) The same-size stones interlock in a variety of ways along this path through a row of plump boxwoods.

- **Determine the pacing.** As much as possible, anticipate the various gaits and strides of the people who will be using the garden on a daily basis. Some people stroll slowly and take small steps, while others move briskly with longer strides. There's also foot size to consider. In general, I use stones that are 12 in. to 18 in. in diameter and space them about 4 in. apart. I often set them in a right-left-right-left pattern to make walking easier. If you're making a garden path for children, the size of stones and distance between them should be smaller than for adults.

- **Foster a sense of seamlessness.** Stepping stones, especially natural stones, look best when they appear as if they could interlock with those next to them—the yang fits into the yin. This creates a feeling of rhythm and cohesion. However, this pattern looks most natural when it is broken once in a while, since there is a random aspect to natural elements.

- **Select an appropriate height for the stones.** If stones are placed within a lawn that will be mowed, place them flush with the lawn. Otherwise set them at least ½ in. above whatever is around them, whether mulch, ground-cover plantings, or bare earth. If they are raised much higher, it might feel precarious to walk on them, especially if the stones are small.

DID YOU KNOW?

The earliest use of stepping stones can be traced to Japan where flat stones provided a slightly raised path surface to keep walkers from getting their feet muddy.

GREEN ROOFS

Even a small gateway can have a living roof, as seen here in this North Carolina woodland. Some of the benefits of green roofs are less water runoff, air purification, oxygen production, and lowered temperature of reflected air. Birds and insects also find cool, private homes in the foliage.

The "green roof" in a North Carolina garden provides shelter for a rustic bench and serves as a gateway along a forest path.

Places to Pause

Every time you stroll through your property, you'll find yourself pausing here and there to do things like taking in the mail, speaking to your neighbor, cutting flowers for the dinner table, or watching birds at the feeder. You take notice of special features such as a change of scenery or view before moving on once more. These are pausing places that signal a short break in the flow. There are three types of places to pause: *gateways* that signal the beginning of a space or a new experience; *landings* that enable us to look down upon a scene; and *turning points* that indicate that some kind of decision should be made.

This front walk offers a natural place to pause before knocking at the front door. The blue British mailbox adds a whimsical touch, while the Adirondack chairs invite visitors to sit awhile.

Gateways

A gateway is an opening that invites you to enter a landscape or garden. It can sit at the edge of your property, dividing outside from inside, or act as a subdivider between gardens. A gateway can be a built entry point such as a portal, a gatehouse, a pair of columns, or a trellis structure, or it can be a natural marker such as two trees framing a view. It can be as spare as an opening in a fence line, or it can have a more three-dimensional presence. Some gateways are actually small rooms, akin to an entry foyer in a house.

When you pass through a gateway, you often feel as though you are embarking upon a special adventure as you enter another realm. Outside the garden is the sidewalk, the roadway, the city, or wilderness—something other than the landscaped realm you have so carefully cultivated. In psychological terms, this cultivated landscape represents a kind of sacred, private place, quite different from the profane, public world outside the garden's walls.

(left) It doesn't take a lot to make a gateway. This gap in a New Hampshire stone wall linked pastures when sheep roamed these hills.

(bottom left) An unusual roofed gateway matches the architecture of the house. With gardens on both sides of the French doors, it's hard to figure if you're inside or out.

(bottom right) The farther you move from house into landscape, the more rustic a gateway can be. This simple garden pergola is left unadorned to weather naturally.

Landings

Landings, or platforms at the head, foot, or middle of a flight of stairs, are transitional spaces where you're invited to rest briefly when you're going up or down stairs. Because it's a place to pause, a landing provides an opportunity to display or feature something that catches the eye. Inside the house, a midpoint landing on the stairs gives you a wall on which to display family photographs or artwork or even to erect a set of bookshelves or install a window seat. Outside, a landing can provide a resting place for looking out onto your property.

Landings are also useful wherever a space narrows down or a change of level occurs. Your front hall or foyer, for example, narrows down to become a hallway that opens out into a more expansive living space. Similarly, your front stoop—a larger, often roofed landing—narrows down to the front walk before it widens again to meet the sidewalk. Why? Because people move like water—they form pools on either side of a restricted channel.

(facing page) A handsome brick landing is the pausing place between the street and the entry to the house.

(below left) It pays to place exterior lights at steps carefully so that they not only light the landing but also the steps themselves.

(below right) The front yard of this narrow Washington, D.C., front yard sits halfway up the slope—a kind of grassy garden landing on the way to the front door.

Many landings serve as transitions between inside and outside spaces. The landing might be as small as a narrow door threshold that offers momentary pause or as big as a vestibule or lobby where a group might assemble before entering the main part of a building. Outside, a large landing could be a porch, a deck, or even a terrace or patio space, which serve as transitional gathering spaces between house and the rest of the yard or garden space. When these exterior spaces are furnished like outdoor living rooms with comfortable chairs and sofas, dining tables, and even outdoor kitchens, they are less about pausing than they are about stopping, the topic of the next section.

Turning Points

Turning points suggest the need for a decision, such as where two or more paths come together at an intersection or a junction. I like to design turning points as circular or square-shaped platforms or individual stones in places where several paths come together.

(above) Like water flowing and pooling along a stream bed, these wide entry steps are contained by a "bank" of handsome retaining walls and large fieldstones from the property.

(above right) In a marriage of materials, the brick front "stoop" and corner steps of this gray-shingled house flow cleanly to meet a landing terrace and half-wall.

(right) This mysterious circular terrace has a spiral form cut into it—a turning point on a grand scale.

Turning points can also act as pausing places along a seemingly endless path: They break up a long path into smaller, more manageable segments. I like to place larger or rounder stepping stones where strollers can, say, enjoy the scent of a rosebush or sit down on a wrought-iron bench set upon a stone landing under a living-room window.

Spaces to Sit

When you finally reach the end of a journey, you're ready to stop and savor things. A stroll through your landscape is no different—you're happy to come to a place where you can sit, relax, and look out onto your property, no matter how big or small it is. Before you begin placing the pieces (the subject of the next chapter), you need to create a good vantage point from which to view what's there, whether you're sitting on a bench in the garden, eating at a picnic table on the lawn, or dining with friends on the terrace.

As we saw in "Places to Be" on pp. 45–47, we are drawn to particular vantage points or outlooks, both inside and outside the house. In this section, we'll explore

(above) The brick walkway resolves the problem of what to do when three paths come together: Make a circle of the same material within the walkway.

(left) Wide concrete steps intersect with a main walkway, forming a natural turning point in the midst of an artful garden room in California.

A JOURNEY THROUGH THE WOODS

Creating a journey through a landscape with winding paths to follow, pauses at events along the way, and stops at destination points is a satisfying way to make a small site feel much bigger than it really is.

North Carolina garden photographer Virginia Weiler and her partner live and garden in a 1950s ranch-style house on a ⅓-acre lot at the end of a cul-de-sac on the outskirts of downtown Winston-Salem. Together with landscape designers Jan Enright and Kevin Lindsey, they crafted a delightful trip

throughout the wooded property, past one event and special feature after another. These include a reflecting water basin, a stone lantern, a celebration tree, Buddha sculptures, and a host of lush plantings.

Stopping places along the route add to the sense of expansiveness. A stone bench for one sits within a woodland planting; a meditation platform for two seems to float several steps above the garden; and a terrace of gravel and weathered pavers provides room for a large group to congregate. Access

to the backyard is along a curving poured-concrete walkway with informal stepping-stone detours that link events to one another. An "infinity path" along the side yard intertwines brick and river stone, combining focal point and walking trail in one. In a far corner of the rear garden awaits a comfortable hammock, nestled under the tree canopy, ready for the hot days of summer and some restful daydreaming.

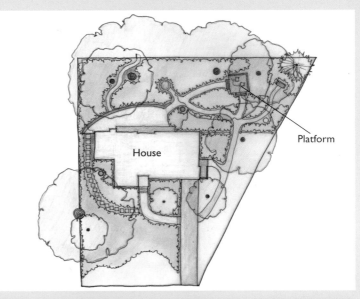

¹ Practically hidden by lush plantings, a diminutive reflecting pool still manages to draw your eye.

² A gazing ball, stone lantern, and red artifact on the gate provide visual interest along the way.

³ A platform in the forest offers a chance to get away.

⁴ A southern tradition is to "trap" evil spirits in bottles suspended in trees.

This vantage point feels like a safe harbor, with a retaining wall that acts as a back to the Adirondack chairs and layers of plantings that screen the terrace from view.

how to design these stopping places in more detail. First, we'll look at how best to site your seating and then how to create hardscapes as vantage points on your property.

Siting Where You Sit

Well-placed seating provides an opportunity to gaze at part or all of a landscape and fully appreciate the setting. Seating that feels inviting and protected encourages people to rest awhile and savor the scene. To ensure that a garden bench—or any other sitting place on your property—looks alluring and encourages you to linger, keep the following three guidelines in mind.

Decide which view you want to enjoy To make outdoor seating as useful as possible, think carefully about where to put it. Walk around the perimeter of your home and throughout the yard and evaluate the various views that are offered. The views might be of a flower garden, a wooded setting, a borrowed distant vista, or a niche where you

might want to place a fountain, a water garden, or a beautifully carved statue. If there is a dynamic focal point—something that is either in motion or that conveys the sense of movement—so much the better.

As I discussed in "Places to Be" on pp. 45–47, there are many perspectives from which to view a landscape. The most common spot for a bench, for instance, is in a cozy corner of a yard, with a long view out onto the surrounding landscape. Another option is to place seating along a path to draw your eyes and feet up or down a hill or on a high point overlooking a distant vista.

Create a sense of security around your bench Once you've determined which view you want to focus on, the next step is to place the seat or bench so that sitting on it is a satisfying experience. The most important thing is to back it up. Imagine the difference between sitting on a backless bench set on an open lawn and on a comfortable teak bench snug against the trunk of a tall shade tree. In the first case,

(facing page) This purple Adirondack chair feels well placed because it nestles up against high plantings at its back.

(above) Whether it's a window seat, a gazebo, or a simple bench, how you site where you sit is critical to whether you'll actually use it.

(left) A deck up in the trees offers an unusual vantage: a high place ("mountain") that feels immersed ("sea").

you perch timidly, checking behind you to make sure no one surprises you from behind. In the second, you can relax into your seat and contemplate the scene because your bench is "backed up."

There are many ways to back up your outdoor seating. You can nestle a bench against a wall, a fence, or a hillside. You can plant large shrubs behind it or a dense bed of ornamental grasses or tall perennials. You can put a bench in a garden house, a gazebo, or a pavilion, or make an arbor or trellis structure overhead to provide shelter from the elements. The backdrop behind the seat serves to create the security and seclusion of a harbor and allows you to forget the outside world as you daydream there awhile.

Relate the seat to its surroundings Like a sofa in a living room, a bench is a piece of furniture in a landscape that needs to work within its context. The closer you locate a seat to a house, the more it should echo aspects of the architecture. For example, a white house with a white picket fence won't look quite right with a rustic twig bench in

(above) In warm climates, it can be a fine line between interior and exterior living. These comfortable wing chairs look as though they belong inside this Santa Fe home.

(right) There's something about this white wrought-iron seat perched atop a handsome stone wall that brings an instant smile to your face. Perhaps it's the skinny legs (shades of Humpty Dumpty?) that make it so delightfully amusing.

the front yard. Better to follow the dictates of the home's design and put a simple white-stained bench there instead. You can also choose the trim color or accent color of your house as the hue for your exterior seating.

On the other hand, the farther away from the house you get, the more rustic your seating can be. Remoteness itself often suggests rusticity. That same twig bench would look great in a woodland setting. A stone slab seat looks wonderful near natural fieldstone walls. However, even this rule begs to be broken. For example, it's fun to come upon a perfect Victorian settee where you least expect it—far into the "wilderness" at the back of your yard.

Pools of Paving

Terraces and patios are gathering places that serve as outdoor rooms—the destination points of our landscape journeys. It's on these carpets of pavers that we congregate to enjoy our backyard. The challenge is to make these hardscapes fit into the landscape without becoming a vast sea of pavement in an otherwise natural setting.

GIVE YOUR BENCH A SOLID FOUNDATION

Even the best-looking outside seating will look unappealing if it is placed off kilter. Always position a bench on a level surface, or change the grade around the bench to create a flat area. If the bench sits along a gravel path, extend the path to form a gravel niche. If there's no existing flat surface to place your seating on, consider making a small terrace or pad. Make the space a little wider than the seat and deep enough to allow a sitter's feet to rest on the floor surface. Cobblestones, bluestone, brick, or flat fieldstone all make handsome terraces for benches.

Some seating can sit happily on a lawn, but I prefer to keep anything wooden from touching the ground by sinking a solid support under each leg. This hidden footing protects your bench from dirt and moisture, even as it appears to sit artfully on the ground.

It's hard to get much more rustic than a bench made out of a fallen log. This one was hewn by hand, with a slightly raised back for a semblance of support.

SUSTAINABLE PAVING

Living lightly involves being aware of the impact your material choices make in the world. Stone paving allows homeowners to create outdoor rooms, terraces, and patios for entertaining, dining, or dancing under the stars. Yet recent trends show that some homeowners are paving over their entire yards with stamped concrete and other impervious materials (garnished with plastic plants) in an effort to cut down on maintenance.

Don't pave paradise completely! Leave cracks or planting pockets or use gravel as the terrace surface. Why? Two reasons: First, adding plant material to hardscaping not only reduces runoff and absorbs heat but also provides habitat for wildlife; and, second, hard surfaces, especially concrete paving materials, look their best when softened by plantings.

When you have a large expanse of pavers, you can soften the effect by "eroding" the edge along the planting bed and replacing some of the interior pavers with plantings.

Start by visualizing a terrace as a pool of space, one that looks best with clean edges softened by plantings or panels of lawn. The edges can be made of cobble or brick "soldiers" stood on end. Or you can use steel edging or let the ends of the pavers themselves serve as edges, as long as the pavers are large enough that they won't move. Here are some helpful hints:

- When making a curved terrace, use wide arcs and cut the pavers to fit.

- With a particularly large expanse of pavers, it helps to pluck some of them out and plant ground covers in the gaps to soften and break up the area into smaller sections.

- Plant billows of perennials or shrubs along the perimeter of a terrace to "settle" it into the landscape. An expanse of concrete pavers, with their man-made patina, needs softening at the edges.

This handsome patio was built from a sandstone driveway that was taken up and then, like a jigsaw puzzle, reworked to become a herb terrace.

- With a terrace of new pavers, it helps to "dirty them up" by sweeping soil over them or, depending upon the hardness of the set, spraying diluted India ink across them.

- Just as inside the house we use different flooring for different rooms—tile for heavy-trafficked areas like mudrooms and bathrooms; soft carpeting for bedrooms and dens; hardwood flooring strewn with area rugs for halls and living areas—outside we can choose various path and terrace surfaces depending on their use.

Ultimately, each of us plays the role of choreographer for the way our visitors perceive and enjoy our personal landscapes. We influence how quickly people walk, what they look at, and how much they savor the events and the stopping places we design for them along the way. In the next chapter, I'll discuss what happens when we *look* closely at our landscape in order to place the pieces just right.

(below left) Granite is an igneous stone, formed from volcanic material that has cooled and become solid. Often, the only plants that can grow on bare rock are crustose lichens, which add an attractive mottled patina.

(below) After moving, pausing, and finally stopping at the destination—here, an Adirondack chair on a front porch—the journeyer can look over the garden and enjoy the colors and textures of spring.

THE MATERIALS UNDERFOOT

You can create a terrace for your home landscape out of a range of materials. Stone offers a handsome and durable surface in a variety of types, sizes, and finishes that only looks better over time. Among the favorite stones for paving are granite, bluestone, limestone, and sandstone—each quarried in a different area of the country. It pays to buy local, as these materials look best where they match the soils around them.

Brick, as blocks of baked clay, is another popular patio material that comes in many hues—red, orange, brown, black, and even blue tones. It can be designed in a host of patterns: common bond, running bond, basketweave, and herringbone, to name a few. Cobblestone—also called "granite setts" in England—is another dimensional material, usually made of granite with rounded edges, used in former times to pave streets. Newer concrete bricks and pavers are inexpensive and readily available, but because they look monolithic if installed over a large area, it pays to break up or soften their edges with plantings.

1 Gravel peastone

2 Natural river stone

3 Bluestone

4 Brick

5 Cobblestone

6 Sandstone

7 Concrete bricks

8 Fieldstone

"A discerning eye needs only a hint, and understatement leaves the imagination free to build its own elaborations."

—RUSSELL PAGE

Placing the Piec

es

Every spring when my children were young, I would drive them to a garden center to pick out materials to create their own little landscape in a corner of our backyard. First, they'd select the plantings—peonies, lilacs, or whatever was in bloom at the time. Then, they'd each choose one small object: maybe a concrete bunny, a painted birdhouse, or a sign with a funny saying. We'd go home and spend the rest of the morning placing these treasures, moving them around until they looked just right. (Inevitably, the actual digging was left to me!) I look back on these spring expeditions as three-dimensional spatial exercises that gave my children on-the-job experience while honing their confidence as designers. They learned early on that you can't randomly set a sundial here or a statue there and expect good results.

There are a number of spatial design principles that will make your property look like a harmonious landscape rather than a backyard jumble. In this chapter, I explain some design concepts that will help you decide where, why, and how to locate the many objects that sit upon your land. When you understand these rules of spatial composition, you'll find that you'll be able to place anything—whether it's something permanent like an outbuilding or a fountain, or temporary like bistro chairs or a grouping of planters.

A Lesson in Spatial Composition

Believe it or not, most of us have an innate understanding of what constitutes good design: We know what looks right when we see it. But when it comes to making aesthetic decisions ourselves, we often freeze because we don't know how, or where, to begin—or we're afraid to make changes or add things that seem so "permanent."

(right) Every object that you bring into your landscape—whether a birdbath or a shrub— needs to be placed thoughtfully.

(bottom left) Your experience placing objects inside your house works just as well outside. Arranging beloved knickknacks on a sideboard or setting a festive table is one way to practice how to position objects on your land.

(bottom right) Every stone you set into your landscape can either look as though it's always been there or it can look out of place. This natural-looking arrangement hugs the ground, echoing the appearance of a stream bed.

Spatial composition is really very simple—it's all about relationships: relationships between you and an object (when you contemplate a statue, for instance), between one object and another (when a bench is placed facing a distant view), or between many objects together (like a grove of trees or a collection of birdhouses).

Take a look at your site. If it's a newly developed property, you'll need to add features to create the landscape that you want. Where you place each new feature in relationship to others is what this chapter is about. If it's an older property, with mature plantings, walls, outbuildings, and other existing elements, you'll need to decide what to keep, what to take away, and what to add to form the landscape that you want.

Auditing Energy

It may sound strange, but the first thing I do when I visit a new property is to perform a kind of mental "energy audit" on the landscape. I'm not talking about

Twin trees frame a handsome urn that sits nestled within a verdant planting. Block out one of the trees with your hand, and you'll instantly see that the energy feels less balanced.

A weeping cherry tree has energy that starts high and moves outward and downward.

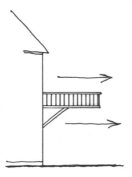

A deck that is cantilevered off the end of a house has strong energy that moves away from the house into the landscape.

A classical statue or clipped topiary sits happily on its pedestal, its energy balanced and complete.

LATENT ENERGY

Each individual element in the landscape—whether a building, a plant, a path, or a view—holds and expresses energy.

(below) You can see abstract patterns of energy in nature as well as in your own backyard. In this landscape, your eye starts at the large stone, follows the curving path of grasses, and moves through the view framed by two small trees.

(facing page) There are two ways to "see" your landscape: in focus, when you observe the details of objects such as the cherry tree in the foreground, or out of focus, when you're aware of the general shape and abstract patterns of groupings of elements like the blurry ball in the background. When you blur the details and see the landscape in the abstract, it's easier to see how to place the pieces.

reviewing the efficient use of electrical energy on a site. What I check for are the "forces"—their direction and magnitude—that radiate from each particular site and the house, vegetation, and landscape elements that sit upon it.

The two homes I grew up in each possessed a different kind of energy. Our first house was a new colonial in a subdivision in Illinois, built on former pastureland. The only feature on the property besides the house was a large maple tree; everything else on our half acre of grass was flat, open, and bland. As you looked out from the house, there was initially nothing to draw your attention or to stop your eye except the edge of the forest beyond the property line. Over the 11 years we lived there, my parents added landscape elements: stone walls, an arbor, a brick patio, a large vegetable garden, a swing set, and a new garage, creating frames and focal points that caught the eye and focused the energies there.

Our next home, sited on a wooded hillside in Connecticut, was a stately house with formal flower gardens built on terraces. Here, the problem was the exact

opposite of our first home: Every space in the large backyard was filled up with flower beds, narrow paths, and overgrown trees so that it all felt chaotic and uncontrolled and too much for a busy family to care for. What we ended up doing was give the property more "breathing room" by turning some of those high-maintenance landscapes back into grass. In both cases, by adding or subtracting elements we found ways to manage the energy to create visually satisfying homes outside.

Seeing in the Abstract

One way to observe the flow of "energy" in and around your property is to see it in the abstract, as an Impressionist painter might. Scrunch up your eyes or remove your glasses or contact lenses so that the different elements lose clarity and look fuzzy. Tall trees become large blobs of green and vertical lines; a flower bed becomes a thick line of color; lawn becomes field; walls turn into dark lines running across the landscape. The view you take in becomes an abstract painting of soft textures, dabs of color, looming volumes, and curving or straight lines that may be altered to suit your aesthetic needs. When you see the landscape as a blur, you focus less on the details and more on the overall forms in front of you. You'll find that you can mentally rearrange blocks of elements with ease, imagining adding a splash here and removing a blob there.

CONDUCT AN ENERGY AUDIT

Walk around your property to observe the flow of energy. Begin by assessing the positive energy. What draws your eye and attracts your attention? How might you best maintain, augment, or embellish upon it? Maybe there's a grand old maple tree in your front yard that's just the right size to shelter your house; a curving flower bed that picks up a similar arc in the circular window over your front door; or a pair of birdhouses that frame the birdbath between them. These are all keepers.

Then assess the negative energy on your site. Where is it coming from and how might you best deflect, block, or break up its influence on the surrounding landscape? Maybe there's a massive house that overwhelms the smaller-scale energy of your home; a confining wall that blocks the natural flow of energy through your site; or a gap in a hedge through which all the energy seems to "bleed out" to your neighbor's yard. These are all items that you need to address in your designs.

(right) A vibrant mélange of colors and textures contrasts sharply with the calm demeanor of this solemn stone focal point set high on a pedestal.

(left) The graceful curve of this concrete statue is highlighted against the thick, clipped hedge behind.

Focal Points and Frames

Placing the pieces in your landscape involves locating both focal points—objects that stand out as the focus of attention—and frames—structures that form a surrounding border or contrasting framework around the objects at hand. You can balance the energy by the way you compose your landscapes through the interaction of focal points and frames.

One way to think about placing the pieces is to imagine your yard as a stage set (the frame) and yourself as the director of a set of actors (the focal points in the landscape that are "performing" there). You get to decide who's the soloist and who's in the chorus; who gets center stage and who steps into the sidelines. In other words, you manage the relationships of the various objects that make up your property, drawing attention to some and allowing others to fade into the background.

FRAMING FOCAL POINTS

Symmetry

The right and left sides of this symmetrical garden arrangement are perfect mirrors of each other. The focal statue stands at the very center on axis with an oblong reflecting pool at her feet. The whole feels complete and balanced.

Asymmetry

The right and left sides in this asymmetrical example are dramatically different yet nevertheless feel balanced. The tall single tree to the left of the statue is complemented by the three large shrubs to the right, and the bend that the path takes to the right adds emphasis to that side.

Within this framework, there are four ways to direct the energy on your site using focal points and frames. I call them the "four Cs": concentrating, connecting, conveying, and containing.

Concentrating Energy with Focal Points

A focal point is something that attracts attention in a landscape. It might be a single object like a statue or a group of objects such as a set of planters on a terrace or birdhouses in a flower border. Focal points stand out from whatever else is around them: They are either a different size, shape, color, or texture, or they catch our eye because they are in motion.

One easy way to place the pieces is to concentrate energy into one or more focal points. You can do this in a number of ways: enthroning, centering, playing with scale, or making it move.

These larger-than-life statues, which represent the Four Seasons, stand out as striking focal points grouped in an informal semicircle in a fern and hosta garden.

FOCAL POINTS:
SETTING OBJECTS IN THE LANDSCAPE

Every object that you bring into your landscape—whether a sun-dial or a shrub—needs to be placed thoughtfully. Focal points add interest to our landscapes by drawing the eye to a certain spot or area. They can be one or more items, or a larger focal grouping. They can also be of different shapes or sizes, as well as of natural or man-made materials.

1. Any solitary vertical object can be a focal point in a backyard landscape.

2. A round concrete ball stands out against a background of spiky plants.

3. This bold red urn is both a focal point and a repeating form aligned with the mountain beyond.

4. One way to arrange focal points is to create an intentional relationship between them.

5. An exuberant figure with raised arms makes a bold statement in a sea of colorful plantings.

6. Water bubbles up from the center of this mill--stone, surrounded by shade-loving plants.

7. If the focal object is a statue, we tend to follow its gaze, noticing what it's looking at.

8. A pair of columns topped with planters forms a gateway that frames the space between.

9. Strong plant forms can be focal points, too, as with these clumps of tufted grasses.

Enthroning Setting an object on a "throne" or pedestal serves to concentrate energy in it. Just as classical sculptors placed marble statues on pedestals, you can enhance the energy of any focal object by raising it above the ground plane on a platform, plinth, or stand. This brings the object closer to eye level or raises it enough that it is silhouetted dramatically against the sky.

Centering Another way to concentrate energy is to place an object in the very center of a landscape, which automatically draws attention to it. You might center a statue or urn between two trees, within an oval or a circle of grass, in a clearing, or in a leftover space in a planting bed. One of my favorite landscape views is of a single bench set under a tree centered in an oval of lawn cut out of an unmown meadow.

(right) When there is a hole to be filled, adding a Japanese lantern at the right scale to the size of the garden provides a strong focal point at the center.

(bottom left) Setting an object on a table, or "throne," helps draw attention to it. If this container were simply on the ground, you might not even notice it.

(bottom right) This striking urn stands out in a large landscape because it is centered on a millstone, which is then encircled by a gently curved retaining wall.

Playing with scale The size of an object makes a big difference in its effectiveness as a focal point in the landscape. Items that are either tiny or huge tend to hold our attention longer than something that's scaled to our own size. If you place a huge object in a small landscape, it grabs our attention. What's surprising is that the same can hold true if you put a tiny object in a large landscape. Its diminutive scale in relation to what's around it makes it stand out from the rest of the landscape.

When you mix big and small together, you can get some surprising results. Some years ago, I designed a tiny urban courtyard garden that needed some focal points. We found two oversize stone rams to place in the little space, but my client was worried that at nearly 5 ft. high they would be much too large for the 20-ft.-square space. I explained that when you put large objects into a small space, the space suddenly feels surprisingly large (see the photo on p. 180). To simulate this effect, I cut out cardboard mock-ups of the sculptures and propped them up where I planned to use them. Seeing the cutouts in place, my client realized that the two larger-than-life-size creatures made the intimate garden feel paradoxically immense.

(above) Tiny sempervivum plants grow in practically no soil in the cracks of a stone wall. Part of the appeal of the composition is the difference in textures; the other is the change in scale.

(left) A teepee's conical form is prominent in any landscape. The scale of this one is a surprise when compared to the relatively small Adirondack chairs placed by its large opening.

(far left) When an object is bigger, or smaller, than you expect it to be, it captures our attention. The tiny hole of this birdhouse made from a stump gives us an idea of its true scale.

PLAYING WITH SCALE

When you place a large element in the foreground and a similarly shaped but smaller element in the background, you carve out space, making it feel larger than it actually is. Conversely, when you place a small object in the foreground and a huge object behind it, you flatten space, making it seem smaller. You can experiment with this idea using one large cardboard box and one small one. Standing in the same viewing position, move the boxes around to test different relationships between them. You'll find that with just two carefully placed objects, you can make your small yard seem immense or your large yard seem intimate.

Like overscaled chess pieces on a game board, these stone rams add focal interest to a shady urban terrace.

Making it move Another way to draw attention to a focal point is to set it in motion. Our house in Vermont looks down over a long meadow onto a round swimming pond surrounded by forest-clad hills that frame the sky. Throughout the course of a day, there's almost always something bringing this natural "garden" to life and attracting our attention. Suddenly the wind will whip up, ruffling the meadow grasses and sending ripples across the pond. Then there are the critters that share the land with us: wild turkeys "bathing" in a dirt pile, porcupines scuttling across the meadow at dusk, chipmunks scurrying across the lawn. On languid summer nights, tiny blinking lights of fireflies resemble the flickering of stars. The constant change offered by these movements animates our landscape and brings us continual delight. While you may not enjoy as much nature around your home as we do, you can bring this same sense of movement to your own backyard by including dynamic focal points in its design.

I recently discovered how essential this type of focal point could be when I was designing the landscape around a contemporary home. To complement the clean, simple lines of the house, we seeded sweeps of lawn, created gracefully curving terraces, and planted orderly groves of trees that look just right against the architecture. But something was missing: It needed a touch of exuberance to counter the restraint.

The garden came alive when we placed a multistemmed crabapple tree—full of dancing, intertwining branches—on the grass terrace. Minutes after it was planted, the tree was engulfed with chirping birds hopping from branch to branch. With the simple addition of an arching tree that attracted wildlife, I had unwittingly created a dynamic focal point and brought a sense of movement into the landscape.

Actual movement The simplest way to bring a feeling of movement to your property is to add in or invite things in actual motion. Moving elements animate a landscape so that you are continually drawn to it, aware of the subtle or dynamic changes constantly taking place. Consider including a fountain, a waterfall, a wind chime, or a bird feeder that attracts birds and other critters.

I have a friend who has a small garden that's always in motion. She looks out through sliding-glass doors across a patio to a wooded knoll where the wind often creates movement in the trees. To heighten the sense of motion, she added a series of objects to catch the light and the wind. The first was a string of twenty 1-in. mirrors that hang from a long, horizontal tree branch. Each mirror catches light throughout the day and casts reflections that travel around the garden as well as inside the house. Then she added silver wind chimes that introduce sound as well as movement. A metallic gazing ball, placed on the ground, completes the dynamic effect.

(above) Focal points in motion are a compelling way to attract attention. This modern sculpture turns in the wind, gently reflecting light as it rotates. Rain falling on the blades causes the sculpture to spin, further animating the shady woodland garden.

(left) The constantly changing quality of light and wind light up this landscape of grasses.

AN OUTDOOR GALLERY

Artist and landscape designer Ketti Kupper transformed a pedestrian-looking property into a modernist landscape of flat surfaces: trays, shelves, landings, seats, and wall hangings of brushed stainless steel, bronze, and concrete. In this "Art Garden," she placed pieces of her own artwork as well as garden elements to create a very personal gallery. From the street edge to the back, this long, narrow property measures only 40 ft. by 132 ft. long, but it is filled with a series of poetic encounters with artwork at every turn.

The first encounter is along the street edge itself, where Ketti artfully placed different pieces in the limited space between curb and sidewalk. A Mondrian-like "dry landscape" of easy-to-maintain pebbles, stones, and grasses is arranged for the enjoyment of passersby. This horizontal work of art is interrupted by a single vertical: a spectacular Angel's Trumpet tree that sits to one side of a central gateway, concentrating the energy between driveway and front walk.

(below) Before the redesign, the front yard had a street view that offered minimal privacy, unwanted noise, and a speck of unused lawn.

Now an Angel's Trumpet tree in bloom gives visual interest to the sidewalk garden.

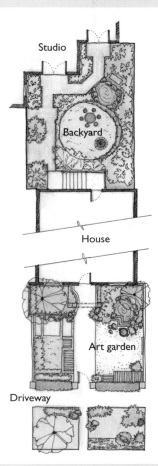

1 "Take all the risks that you want" is the message that greets visitors as they push open the garden door.

2 Concrete slabs lead from the driveway to the front walk. Ahead, a panel called "Five Graces" focuses our attention on the weathered steel wall.

3 In the backyard, the circular form of the grass underfoot is repeated in each of the permanent elements placed there: a chiminea, a table, and six stools.

Studio

Backyard

House

Art garden

Driveway

The wooden gate set between thick stucco piers signals entrance into the owner's private realm. Inside is an outdoor living space that's like a decompression chamber from the outside world. Flat concrete and wood viewing benches look onto vertical plaques composed of images and words of varying scales, each with a deliberately ambiguous meaning. For instance, an overscaled photograph of a running woman wearing sneakers declares, "Go. Meet Yourself." Nearby, a tiny plaque on the door into the garden states, "Take all the risks that you want."

Ketti designed her works of art to integrate both with the architecture and with the landscape. Three have a teal-gray color scheme similar to the house and pillars. One, an abstract silvery panel entitled "Five Graces," is set against a backdrop of twinkling hillside lights at night and the patina of rusted steel during the day. This outdoor room feels museumlike with its focal points hung on walls, yet it's unmistakably a garden, edged with natural stones matched to silver-leafed plantings that spill across the clean lines of concrete edging.

1 A vine-covered walkway takes you past an outdoor workspace and ends at Ketti's studio with its chartreuse arched door.

2 The same artistic sensibility is evident both inside and out. A well-placed mirror adds light to a short hallway, reflecting the garden.

3 This sliding door off the driveway opens up to reveal an art piece with the title "Go. Meet Yourself."

(above left) Both light and wind bring movement to these colorful ornaments—the light bounces off their curving surface at odd angles and the wind lifts them in a breeze.

(above right) Spirals bring a sense of movement to a static object, like this unusual planter. Your eye can't help but follow the whirling line.

Implied movement As with the twisting and twining branches of the crabapple tree in my client's garden, implied motion can be nearly as effective as actual movement in creating a dynamic garden. The still water of a reflecting pool acts as a mirror for the ever-changing patterns of clouds. A weeping willow, known as the "waterfall tree" in our family, provides a virtual cascade of branches. We follow the gaze of an overscaled statue staring out from a corner, feel the upward-thrusting energy of a spiral form, or peer through a framed opening to a distant vista. The experience of moving mentally through a garden or climbing its vertical focal points in our mind's eye is essential to making a static space come alive.

Connecting Focal Points

Another way to manage the energy on or around your property is to connect objects to each other as a means of bringing harmony to the whole. Your eye can pick out relationships more easily if you repeat elements or make collections in your backyard landscapes. Stones can also be useful in connecting different parts of your garden.

Repeating elements The easiest way to connect the energy both in and around your house is to repeat an element: a color, a texture, a shape, or even a style. When you do this, you create an automatic connection between the elements that stand out in a landscape of otherwise unrelated objects.

Children enjoy "connecting the dots" by drawing a line from one numbered dot to the next to reveal a picture that couldn't otherwise be deciphered. In a similar way, you can connect focal objects to each other and unveil a larger pattern by repeating an element and uniting different areas. Similarly shaped clay pots filled with flowering plants that encircle an entry court, the same conical evergreen used in different corners of the yard, or a teak bench that you find inside and outside of the house all bring a sense of unity and order to your landscape design.

Inside the house, you repeat elements when you place colored throw pillows on a couch that match one of the chair cushions in the same room. Outside, you might relate the triangular shape of your eave to a similarly shaped clipped yew in your front yard. If you live in a log home, you might echo the timber styling in your choice of outdoor furniture. Repeating an element can help restore order to a chaotic landscape and bring harmony and a sense of balance to the whole property.

Making collections   Another way to connect focal objects is to make a collection out of them. In one area of your property, you might select only plants of a particular species, such as daylilies, ferns, or palms. In another area, you might set out a grouping of different-colored gazing balls, each with similarly hued plantings beneath them. Or, like my mother, you could collect old gardener's gloves and place each one

(above) The warm tones of the chair pillows echo those of the daylilies in this inviting front yard. Repeating an element draws the eye to make connections between objects in a landscape.

(left) Using a limited palette of colors brings harmony to a small space. The brightness of the chartreuse door is repeated in the plantings around it, contrasting with the earthen tones of the architecture.

on its own picket to adorn an old fence. Collections are satisfying because they contain a range of objects with similar attributes that connect parts of a landscape to each other as you move around the property. In fact, on a larger scale, sculpture gardens are really collections of objects united by the curator's vision and set out along a path.

Using stones as focal points Setting stones into your landscape is another way to connect one part of a garden to another. Whether you are setting a few large rocks within a planting or arranging a backyard waterfall, keep the following principles in mind so the stones look as though they belong. As you get into the practice of setting stones in place, you may find yourself transported back to the delights of your childhood sandbox, only with larger elements to capture your attention.

- **Look to nature first before placing stones.** Study landscapes and landforms such as ledge outcroppings, stream beds, waterfalls, rocky coastlines, and stony islets and

When stones are set well, you can't tell whether they were set there by nature or by hand.

use them as your guide. Note the natural patterns of your local stone as it sits in the ground. Limestone, for instance, has horizontal striations, so set it parallel to the ground rather than vertically on edge.

- **Make sure that your stones are set firmly into the earth.** This means that you want to set them to their "knees" (about one-third of the way up from their "feet," or bottom of the rock) or their "waist" (about halfway up from their feet). If you allow the underside of a rock to be exposed, it will look as though you simply plopped it down.

- **Establish a relationship between or among stones.** With two stones, make the larger rock the major or dominant stone, and a smaller rock the minor or subordinate stone. It helps to conjure up an image for the relationship between stones—a "mother/child" pairing, for instance, or one of leaning and supporting. When placing three or more stones, create a triangular relationship among them, such as a tall "standing" stone, a

(below left) Setting stones is infinitely easier with the help of a large excavator or crane. To create an aesthetic composition that doesn't look like a pile of rocks, make sure you have a clear image in mind before you begin.

(below right) Two verticals—the statue with upraised arm and the columnar evergreen in the background—contrast strongly with the horizontal stone bench and the curving path that leads to it.

SETTING STONES

Yes

No

(above left) Stones look natural when softened by plantings, set into mosses, or floated on a bed of gravel.

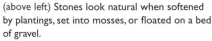

(above right) Three thoughtfully positioned stones form a focal grouping in a sea of poppies. When you set three objects together, you create a balanced triangular relationship, one that may be equilateral (if set with the same spacing between each one) or scalene (asymmetrical).

medium-size flat-topped stone, and a low "lying" stone. However many stones you set, it helps immensely to have an image firmly in mind before you begin.

- **When lining a stream or planting bed, use stones of different sizes.** Think of how rocks look at the edge of a stream; they either pile up through deposition or are swept away through erosion. Smaller stones tumble to the side of larger rocks, varying the depth and height of the shoreline. In your landscape, as in nature, lining up stones that are all the same size looks stiff and contrived.

Conveying Energy into the Landscape

There are times when you don't want to concentrate energy or collect it, but instead choose to convey, or transmit, that energy outward into the landscape. Conveying energy is useful when an object feels particularly forceful, such as a deck that juts way out into the backyard or when you'd like to "spread" the energy around, as with an overgrown tree that sits too close to the house. There are two useful techniques for doing this: creating visual breathing room and employing the ripple effect.

Visual breathing room Just as we all need a certain amount of personal space to feel comfortable in a crowd, an object, whether a birdbath in the backyard or a house in the landscape, often benefits from some visual breathing room, or a zone of open space around it.

Imagine that a house has fallen forward onto its front facade. The imprint it leaves is usually the right amount of level ground needed for a garden, patio, or lawn. A similar approach can be applied to a birdbath, a fountain, or any other round or squat object. In all these cases, the space around the object draws attention to it and gives it room to breath. Around a house without gutters, you can give visual breathing room to the structure while draining water off the roof by creating a drip line

MOCK IT UP

Before you apply the ideas about placing the pieces in your landscape, it's a good idea to try them out on a small scale first, practicing right on your dining-room table. Here's how:

Pretend the table is your property. Set out boxes to represent the house and outbuildings, paper cones for important trees, ribbons for paths, and strips of cardboard for enclosures. (Or use anything close at hand.) This is where you can be adventurous and spend plenty of time rearranging before actually making any real changes. You can practice all the compositional techniques mentioned so far: concentrating, connecting, or conveying energy. Add new elements or move around the existing ones. Placing the pieces in miniature is a fun exercise for the family to do together, while enabling you to envision and test out some of the design ideas and changes you'd like to make in your yard.

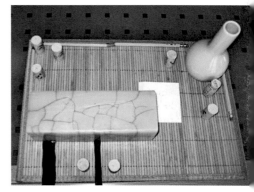

A vase, wine corks, a candle, and pencils on a placemat represent landscape design elements, which are easy to rearrange before you start digging.

(left) This ancient maple tree needs some breathing room around it, not only for the health of its root system but also for visual appeal. The shape of the handsome stone retaining wall mimics the drip line of the tree's canopy.

(right) Frames are found in nature and in a designed landscape. Here, two tall trees frame a view of a mountain ridge, while at their feet a smaller twig gateway performs the same function, only at a more human scale.

(far right) A stone arch frames a raft floating on a swimming pool.

A house has a lot of latent energy. One way to disperse that energy into the landscape is to use concentric rings that ripple out from the house. Here, a semicircular motif is repeated in the deck, the retaining walls, and the lines of the terrace.

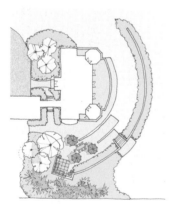

outside the perimeter of the foundation (see the drawing on p. 55). Install a clean edge of granite, steel, or wood and infill with gravel or peastone from the foundation out to the drip edge .

The ripple effect Just as there are ways to concentrate energy in the landscape, there are also ways to disperse it. One of these is to create a ripple effect. When you drop a pebble into a still pool, concentric waves of water ripple outward, decreasing in intensity until they meet the shore. Similarly, when you place an object in your landscape, its energy can dissipate into the objects and space around it. You make a simple ripple effect around specimen trees or shrubs when you plant ground covers or rake gravel at their bases. A more intricate ripple effect would involve planting in concentric rings around a focal point.

Frames: Containing Energy

A frame is a structure that encloses or contains the energy of a particular space. You look at—or through—frames all the time, both inside and outside your house. When you frame a painting, you mount it into a decorative border that finishes the raw edge of the canvas. When you edge your garden bed, you create a spaded border that makes it look neat and orderly. Area rugs are often designed with a contrasting border that frames the design within it. Windows and doors have trim boards around the casings that frame the views out to the landscape. By making frames around the objects or areas that you want to feature, you set them off as distinctive, different, or unusual. There are two kinds of frames that you can form in your landscape: vertical frames and horizontal frames.

Vertical Frames

Every window in your home offers an opportunity for framing the energy of a view. Whether casement window or sash, each opening is a frame that punctures a vertical wall, bringing the background into focus. Even sliders, French doors, and ganged windows (windows grouped together as a set) can be thought of as two- or three-paneled paintings of our backyard landscapes.

Designing the frame   The design properties of each window in your house affect the way it frames the view—and the energy—beyond it. Changing the color of the window frame, for instance, alters the relationship of foreground to background. White trim stands out as distinct from the landscape it frames, emphasizing the architecture of the window wall rather than the background landscape. Clear-stained wood frames or those painted a dark color such as forest green tend to blend in with the landscape beyond, so the natural background becomes one with the foreground

These windows are "ganged" together as a unit, so that the landscape beyond is segmented into parts, making it feel like an ever-changing landscape painting on the wall.

HIDE AND REVEAL

Landscape designer Maggie Judycki has created a backyard oasis in her small suburban lot outside of Washington, D.C., which is set in a neighborhood of ranch houses and colonial-style homes built in the late 1960s. Her property opened onto several neighbors' yards, but rather than walling herself off completely, Maggie decided to hide the less attractive parts and reveal others by means of thoughtful framing.

In one case, Maggie highlighted a red maple tree by designing a new stone wall in the shape of a half circle directly on center with it. She then clipped its crown into a matching semicircle and installed a bamboo screen just behind the trunk to regain privacy. The effect is quite magical—the curve of

the tree is reflected by the curve of the wall with both halves forming a full circle in the process. The two very different materials join as one, making a wonderful focal point in her backyard landscape.

Maggie also chose to reveal a particularly lush part of another neighbor's garden, while hiding the house from view. She used standard 6-ft.-high stockade fencing along the back boundary of her property but lowered it to 3 ft. to allow the view she desired, so that it lined up with her attractive stone terrace and is overlooked by her living-room windows. In such a small property, achieving greater depth by borrowing a view adds immeasurably to your enjoyment of the home outside.

(right) The semicircular form of the carefully pruned maple with slatted screen behind delights the eye, gives privacy, and echoes the form of the wall.

(below) Cutting through the wall.

A segment of this stockade fence is cut down to a lower height to "borrow" the view of the neighbor's property, giving greater depth to this narrow backyard.

frame. Playing with the color of your window frame or sash can marry foreground to background in many different ways.

The "picture window" of the 1950s—a broad sweep of glass that filled almost an entire wall—was meant to bring the landscape indoors. Thanks to new developments in glass manufacturing, these massive windows were created without any subdivisions whatsoever and often occupied a focal position in a living room. By contrast, windows with multiple panes, such as colonial New England's traditional "six over six" windows, subdivide the background into separate parts that segment the view. Each part of the view becomes an abstraction of the whole.

The vertical frame doesn't have to be a window, of course. Screened porches, with their removable screens, also segment the view into parts, as do the columns of roofed porches. A pergola is a landscape structure with posts as vertical frames and a latticework roof above, designed to support climbing vines. Less formal are arbors—structures made of latticework that support plants or vines—that offer framed views onto an ornamental garden. Twin tree trunks can frame a distant view. You can even

(below left) Inside and outside can be seen as one when the color scheme is coordinated. Here, the hydrangea bush outside the window relates to the apple green of the striped pillow inside. The green also complements the deep purple of the seat cushion, and the warmth of the tawny hillside is seen again in the wall and floor color.

(below top right) With a wide picture window, it can be hard to distinguish inside from outside. In this cheery sunroom, beloved objects create an inviting place to relax with a book, while the panoramic view beyond is framed nicely for watching boats on the river.

(below bottom right) By contrast, the view through a sash window with divided muntins is much more segmented, which can still be interesting in its own right.

turn a fence into a frame by removing some of the slats, as we did for a client whose house overlooked Lake Michigan.

Horizontal Frames

We not only use frames on walls and in the air but also on the ground. Inside the house, a wood parquet floor may be edged with a band of a different-colored wood that calls attention to the interior pattern. In our vegetable gardens, we place vertical boards to create raised beds that retain improved soils, keep weeding to a minimum, and provide a handsome background pattern for the vegetables that are grown there. Sometimes we even edge our lawns, turning them into grass panels in a geometric shape, framed by steel or stone edging. By surrounding a space with a border or edging, we contain its energy, making what's inside look more cared for and better appreciated, and, as a result, it seems to take on more value. A horizontal frame that defines and edges a space brings a sense of calm and clarity to a landscape.

(left) The entry to the author's house has a strong "mouse-hole effect," drawing the visitor in toward the light and the view. As an additional attraction, the deep-purple wall contrasts strongly with the bright southern light in the dining room beyond.

(facing page) You can create a sense of expansion and depth in the smallest of spaces by using horizontal lines to subdivide the space into layers.

THE MOUSE-HOLE EFFECT

When you shrink the size of an opening, what's behind it seems to become more significant. It's the same effect as when you look through a telescope or a porthole on a ship: The world is reduced to just what's inside the frame. Because the frame is small, you contemplate what's in view and notice every detail. This effect works best with a limited number of openings in an otherwise solid wall. A form of the hide-and-reveal idea discussed on p. 148, mouse holing is a little like playing peek-a-boo with the viewer: Now you see it (the view), now you don't. You can use a mouse hole as a kind of tease, giving little tastes along the way until the whole opens up to view at a wider vantage point. If you can actually walk through a mouse hole, the effect becomes even more powerful.

You don't need a distant landscape to frame a worthy view. This round cutout in a pink wall directs our gaze on the delightful Euphorbia plants it frames.

Receiving forms You can also use walls, edging, and other frames to contain energy that is spilling outward from a particularly dynamic form. A deck that juts into the yard or a swimming pool that thrusts outward at an odd angle to the house benefits from the addition of a "receiving form" to capture and contain the energy that emanates from it. The receiving form for the jutting deck might be a U-shaped sitting wall; for the pool, it might be a fence that sits kitty-corner to the odd-angled thrust, stopping its energy from bleeding out into the neighbor's yard. Think of it as the yin (something concave) to the yang (something convex) in the landscape.

Foreground, middle ground, and background Another kind of horizontal framing occurs when you relate the foreground landscape to the background view by means of something in between—the middle ground. At our house, for example, we created a foreground lawn area right outside our basement playroom that is retained by a 4-ft.-high wall. Along the curve at the top, I planted a border of colorful peren-

Like a picture window on the ground, this horizontal frame surrounds a pool of shallow water that reflects the sky.

(left) If part of your house juts into the landscape, be it a cantilevered deck or the covered porch shown here, building a wall in the corner of the property helps to "receive" and contain its energy. The lawn allows an appropriate amount of breathing room.

(below) In this layered arrangement in a quiet corner of a patio, the watering can is not only functional but also becomes part of the composition.

nials and ornamental grasses. Below the wall lies a field—the middle ground—edged by an old apple orchard with forest beyond. In the distance—the background—lies a view of hills and open fields some five miles away. These three planes act as successive horizontal frames in space. The effect is to underscore the distant view, while "capturing" it and making it feel as though it is far closer than it actually is.

While not everyone has a distant view like ours, you can create the same effect by subdividing your backyard into a foreground, a middle ground, and a background. The foreground might be your terrace or deck, edged by a sitting wall or railing. The middle ground might be a play space of lawn. The background might be a line of shrubs and trees, with a specimen tree or sculptural object standing out as a focal point. This creates a kind of ripple effect in your landscape, collapsing or expanding space, and giving your land a sense of order, interest, and energy that moves outward from the house to the edge of the property and back again.

Once you've tried out the ideas in this chapter on your tabletop—playing with space by placing the pieces and moving them around until they feel right—you'll have the confidence to move outside to your land and try it full scale. The results may surprise you. Managing the energy when you concentrate, connect, convey, or contain focal points and frames, you'll quickly become skilled at spatial composition. When you place the pieces just so, you'll find yourself transforming your home outside into a personal work of landscape art.

The next chapter focuses on the sensory pleasures that we derive from living on our land. When we craft the details, we express something about ourselves using materials from nature. How can we design our landscapes so that all the elements "sing" in harmony? As writer Henry David Thoreau said, "This world is but canvas to our imaginations." So, too, is the land where we live.

CAPTURING THE VIEW

If you follow a maple-lined lane to its very end, you'll come to a little farmhouse on a hill, complete with a stone-edged herb garden at its feet. The house sits surrounded by fields and forests, enjoying an occasional peek-a-boo view out to distant mountain peaks. The owners had lived in the old Cape for many years before deciding to build an addition to house themselves and their growing extended family. Our firm was asked to help guide improvements to their landscape and make sense of the new relationships between house and land, creating a new driveway, entry terrace, and gardens.

Making the most of the existing features was the first important task. To call attention to a statuesque maple that stood as the focal point of the new addition, we created an upper viewing terrace around it, composed of big chunks of granite loosely set with herbs and low perennials sewn into the cracks. Another key existing feature was the owner's vegetable

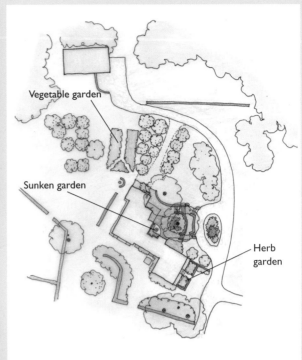

Vegetable garden

Sunken garden

Herb garden

[1] The herb garden in front of the original farmhouse is edged by old granite curbing.

[2] A lone white birch, an accident of nature, stands out from this stately line of ancient sugar maples that lead to the farmhouse.

[3] A natural cut in the forest affords a glimpse of a distant mountain peak, echoed in the form of the urn.

garden, a long, rectangular space that had been gardened for more than 25 years. By tweaking the garden's borders to bring them in line with the new addition and centered on a break in the trees, we were able to capture a distant view and make it the focal point of the garden. We then placed a handsome urn on its own pedestal to repeat the form of the mountain peak and underscore its importance in the landscape.

[1] The curved terrace reflects the drip line of an old sugar maple at the entrance to the new addition.

[2] A grass path aligned with the red urn bisects the vegetable garden.

[3] A millstone fountain sits as the centerpiece of the small sunken garden, the focal point nestled between two entryways.

Sensory Pleasur

As homeowners, we each express our personality through the choices we make throughout the process of design. What "big move" we choose, when we enjoy the different "comfort zones," how we make our landscape "flow," and where we place the pieces all require big decisions so that the end result works. Yet it is our selection of details and final flourishes that truly gives a space a particular life and feeling. The materials, colors, and details we use set a mood and give the flavor for who we are and how we live in our home outside. Just as your choice of wall color, tile design, furniture style, or upholstery fabric expresses something about how you live your life inside your house, your choice of exterior house color, outdoor furniture style, and paving and porch materials presents a particular picture as to what you love outside. How you arrange plants, decide on lighting fixtures, and incorporate water features in your home outside all give sensory pleasure to your daily life. Being outside on your land brings you closer to nature and stimulates each one of your senses.

"Acts of creation are ordinarily reserved for gods and poets. To plant a pine, one need only own a shovel."

—ALDO LEOPOLD

In this chapter, I talk about the sensory pleasures you get from paying attention to the details of your home outside. I offer some easy-to-use design ideas that help you make decisions about how to deploy the details you choose. Much like the way you put together an outfit every day, choosing harmonious colors, textures, and patterns—matching tie to socks, belt to purse—you can put together the materials for your landscape with similar flair. These exterior finishes provide the final flourishes that "sing," the spices that bring the flavor of home outside to the fore. I like to think of them in terms of the most fundamental natural elements—earth, water, fire, and air.

Pleasures of the Earth

To state the obvious, the Earth is essential to our everyday survival. Not only is it the planet we inhabit, but it is also the land on which we live, build, and walk, and the soil in which plants grow. In this section, we explore the fundamentals of planting

In this summertime scene, climbing roses, green flowering tobacco, and purple ageratum light up an evergreen boxwood hedge.

design, so that you can begin to incorporate these earthy delights more confidently into your home outside.

Thus far, I have avoided focusing on specific plants, since this is a book about home landscaping rather than specifically about gardening. But since plants are such an integral part of the home outside, I will address them in more detail now. Because not all plants can grow in every region, you may not recognize all the species that are pictured here. For this reason, I have chosen to identify them by their common name, using Latin nomenclature only when no common name exists. My hope is that, by using the planting design ideas I discuss, combined with substitutions for the specific plants noted, you'll be able to create a beautiful planted paradise on your own.

Seasonal Change

Plants provide us with a host of sensory pleasures—shade, scent, taste, texture, color, and visual delight—and are a vital component of the home outside. A big part of the

(top) In spring, clouds of white crabapple blossoms burst forth, intoxicating the senses.

(bottom left) Virginia creeper turns scarlet in the fall, encouraged by the warmth that radiates from this New England stone wall.

(bottom right) In this garden, the cock crows, no matter what the season. With the right details in place, a garden in winter can be just as beautiful as every other time of year.

WATERING TIPS

When plants are first put in the ground, they need to be well watered to establish healthy root systems. The best time to water is when the sun is not out so as not to burn the leaves. (A droplet of water acts as a mini magnifying glass.) With the right plant in the right place, minimal watering should be necessary. Selecting plants native to your region and thus adapted to your environment will also reduce excess water use while providing the additional benefit of bringing the natural landscape into your own small piece of the world.

Fountain grass and purple cone-flower—an herb used to stimulate natural resistance by helping maintain the immune system—arch over a path.

pleasure of using plants in your landscape is the element of change. In northern climates, after a long winter, when deciduous plants lie dormant and evergreens maintain their leaves or needles, early spring brings much-needed color to the home outside. Early blooming perennials, like Christmas rose, can blossom in the snow. Daffodil bulbs, planted in the fall, peek out through the mud of early spring, brightening a gray landscape with splashes of yellow and white. Late spring into early summer is the climactic moment for a home garden, when many trees, shrubs, and perennials present their showy blooms. Mid- to late summer enjoys a quieter period when annuals—those plants that flower, produce seed, and then die, all in one season—augment the blooming period of the garden. In fall, the garden begins to fade, except for a few hold-out perennials such as sedum, asters, and chrysanthemum. The leaves of deciduous shrubs and trees start turning colors, eventually dropping to leave behind denuded skeletal structures throughout the long, bleak winter.

The rhythm of the seasons is best lived by being out of doors in your landscape, as you plant, tend, and find pleasure in the trees, shrubs, and ground covers that you install there.

Getting Started

Most American houses sit on an expanse of lawn stretching from foundation to street, overtopped by a single shade tree with maybe a sprinkling of trees, shrubs, and annuals around the edge of the building. But with a little research and a few rules of thumb (preferably a green one), it's really not that hard to turn your yard into a beautifully planted landscape. Here's how:

- **Get inspired** by visiting parks, gardens, arboreta, and nurseries to become acquainted with the vast variety of plants that grow in your region. Go back often to observe how they develop over time—when they leaf out, when and how their flowers bloom, and how they develop their fall color and how they look in winter. Notice the shape and size of trees, shrubs, and perennials, and how they look in combination with other plantings. Use this information, bolstered by conversations with gardener friends and local horticulturists or by doing Internet research, to bring your favorite plants to your own landscape.

- **Learn your soil type.** As discussed on p. 29, take soil samples from several areas around your property and send them to your local county extension service for testing. In return, you will receive recommendations on what to use to augment the quality of your soil for the best planting results.

This garden uses the right plants in the right places to minimize the need for irrigation. Reducing water usage where possible will help sustain one of Earth's increasingly scarce resources.

COLOR IN THE GARDEN

When you combine plants to create a garden, you learn a lot about color. Here are some combinations to consider as you decorate your landscape with the vast range of perennials and annuals available on the market.

1 A cottage garden border.

2 Salmon-hued impatiens, an annual that works well in deep shade, melds well with the peachy color of the walls of the house.

3 Stargazer lilies.

4 Red bee balm combines with a range of greens to create a harmonious grouping.

5 Placing various values of blues and purples near each other enhances the value of each.

6 The lime green flowers of lady's mantle look exquisite against blue perennial geraniums, rose-colored alliums, and pink shrub roses.

7 The limey color of euphorbia contrasts with the blue-green tones of eucalyptus.

8 Russian sage, purple coneflower, and the towering pinky-red flowers of joe-pye weed are tried-and-true plants that work well together in a range of conditions.

• **Mock up your planting beds** by setting out hoses or flags or by spraying water-soluble paint, then checking how your designs look from inside the house and from different vantage points on your property. A good size for a planting bed ranges from 4 ft. to 8 ft. wide. Anything narrower looks thin; anything deeper requires an interior path for maintenance purposes.

• **Dig out your planting beds** to a depth of 12 in., adding in the suggested amendments and compost as you go. Good friable—easily worked—soil is one key to happy plantings.

• **Set plants in the right place.** Check your sun/shade diagrams from p. 24. Some plants need full sun to thrive, while others do well in part shade. Plant tags give pertinent information about the hardiness zone, spacing, depth of planting, and the height the plant is expected to grow.

Plant a host of tall perennials in beds that define a sunny square of lawn to create an exuberant pleasure ground on your property.

This standout tree serves many functions: It brings shade to an otherwise sunny part of the garden, provides structure for a climbing vine, and acts as an archway along a winding path.

- **Move plants around** until you get them right. Most plants are forgiving creatures. They are happy to be dug up, divided, or moved from one place to another. Because plants grow and change over time, your landscape looks best when you spend a few hours a week tending it.

Making the Most of Trees in the Garden

The first plants to install in your landscape are those that have the greatest impact—namely, trees. Each tree brings many facets to a home landscape, creating canopy, shade, structure, framing, and of course, a natural climbing structure. Planting a tree is one of the boldest things you can do on your property. For one thing, you're choosing the location of a prominent and long-lived plant and one that's not so easily moved once established. Even a single tree can change the microclimate of your yard over a relatively short time, often determining the scale and growth conditions for other vegetation.

ADD THREE TREES

Planting a few trees to either side of a house with minimal vegetation settles it into the landscape, softens the architecture, and brings privacy to those who live there.

Most of us have limited space for planting anything as large as a tree. To choose what to plant and where, it pays to think about trees in relationship to one another and to the other plantings in a garden. A good place to start is to identify the existing trees on your property (see p. 29). Sketch a working site plan and record the location of all significant trees. Then make a list of your favorite trees and research their size, growth habit, and hardiness zone to make sure they are good candidates. Next, think about how existing and future trees, whether placed individually or within groups, might enhance the mood and structure of your garden.

Feature a standout tree Do you have a standout tree on your property? In garden design terms, such a tree is known as a specimen, an individual tree that's planted for its distinguishing ornamental or symbolic qualities. On our property, we have a huge specimen oak, which probably provided shade for the sheep that roamed the land many years ago. It stands alone, shading our house and supporting an old tire that swings out boldly over the sloping ground.

A standout tree doesn't have to be large to make its presence felt. This tree fans out across the white stucco wall of a contemporary house.

(far left) You can create a processional allée—an alleyway—in your backyard by simply planting the same species of tree or shrub opposite each other along a path. Make sure to include a focal point at the end.

(left) A stepping-stone path through an oak grove leads to a series of clearings—one for a wooden bench and the other for a cabin.

A standout tree doesn't have to be large: The delicate dance of a well-pruned cut-leaf Japanese maple can pack as much punch as a towering copper beech. And you can have more than one specimen tree in a garden, but they should be placed so that each stands out within its own realm.

Groves and clearings If you have a wooded area on your property, it might feel like a tangle, a wild thicket, or just an amorphous shaded haven. With some thoughtful pruning, you can re-create the feeling of a forest in your own backyard.

Whether a bamboo grove, a cathedral pine wood, or a rain forest jungle, clusters of trees in a natural setting are typically composed of three parts: a stand of trees, trails that cut through the trees, and occasional clearings or glades that let in light and air. With this in mind, take on your backyard wilderness with your loppers or pruning shears to make it habitable. Cut out a meandering path that leads to a small clearing, placing a twig bench or some perching stones there.

When composed of many species, a grove feels natural, like the mixed woodland around our home in Vermont. In a city or suburb, where mixed woodlands are less common, I re-create them using a mix of deciduous and coniferous trees and shrubs when installing perimeter plantings to give privacy to a home. This simulation of a natural grove encloses the property in a way that feels natural and offers a range of textures, colors, and flowering times throughout the year.

Create a sense of order with formal arrangements Ordered stands of trees are typically of a single species, like an orchard or an Italian *bosco*—a small grove designed to fit the size constraints of a garden. Mazes, parterres, and formal garden rooms require a strict geometric pattern for planting the trees or shrubs that create the desired form. Along the perimeters of a path, an ordered grove of trees becomes an allée, an avenue, or even a tunnel (see left photo above).

Layer in a mix of deciduous and evergreen trees from lowest in front to highest in back to add a sense of depth along the perimeter of a small property.

Formal plantings usually look best when they are visually related to the geometry of your house; for example, the lines of an orchard could be parallel or perpendicular to the lines of your house. But sometimes it's fun to create a sudden surprise on your property: a "fairy circle" of trees planted within the "wilderness" at the scruffy back corner of your lot. Having something perfect within an imperfect setting can bring the excitement of the unexpected to your backyard.

Working with Shrubs

Shrubs can be used in a host of forms to add another dimension to your landscape. One way to plant them is in informal groupings with grasses, herbs, perennials, and even vegetables to create a mixed collection known as a "cottage garden"—the kind of unstructured plantings you might find in front of a small house in the country.

A garden spills down a handsome stone path to meet the sidewalk. Mixing shrubs with perennials, bulbs, and grasses enables you to plant—and move things around—with abandon.

You can also use shrubs to enclose, frame, and layer your landscape. Some bushes, such as yews, privet, or boxwood, can form a dense hedge that can be clipped by hand or sheared with an electric trimmer to make a vegetal wall, an openwork screen, or a time-intensive pruned "espalier" that is trained to grow flat against an upright surface. Japanese gardeners employ shrubs to create a "trimming line" or low hedge that is pruned to become the lowest leg of a frame for a middle-ground or distant view. You can even plant a range of evergreen and deciduous shrub species together that you prune as a mixed hedge that comes in and out of bloom at different times of the year.

Shrubs can function as focal objects in a landscape. Pruned as spheres or topiaries—bushes or trees trimmed into decorative shapes such as oversize animals or chess pieces—shrubs can captivate the viewer just as any good sculpture can. Plant them in drifts, billows, or odd-numbered groupings for maximum effect.

Shrubs can be used in many ways within a single garden. Here, they are used alone as punctuation points along the path, pruned together as one planted wave, and encircle the cherry tree and bench in the background.

JEWEL IN THE CROWN

On a side street near downtown Akron, Ohio, a handsome Victorian sits high above the street, a jewel in the city. It wasn't always that way. When landscape designers Samuel Salsbury and Sabrena Schweyer bought this house more than 15 years ago, it sat on a lawn with an oak tree as its sole planting. The back of the property was even more dismal, with a chain-link fence to one side, a debris-strewn garage to the other, and a derelict house beyond.

Over the years, Samuel and Sabrena have landscaped every inch of their grounds. Today, passersby are delighted by the upward-sloping front garden, packed to the gills with a colorful mix of perennials, shrubs, bulbs, and ground covers that spill across the sidewalk to the street. A plant-filled front porch greets arriving visitors.

The backyard is a planted haven for dining alongside a cascading stream that meanders between favorite statues.

This in-town, turn-of-the-century home looked down upon an undistinguished front lawn. Now, abundant plantings have overtaken the front lawn and sidewalk strip, enveloping the house with a rich variety of forms, colors, and textures.

There's room for a vegetable garden in one sunny corner, and a sliver of land along the driveway makes the perfect cutting garden, filled with daylilies and other brightly colored perennials. At the back corner of the property, by that once derelict garage, you can look back through layers upon layers of beautiful plantings and feel that you've found a tiny patch of paradise.

[1] Set in the back corner of a shady urban bower, an old-fashioned tea party awaits its guests.

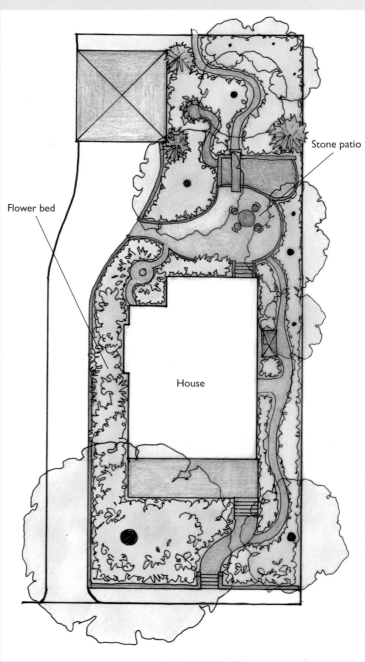

Flower bed

Stone patio

House

Tiny pinpoints of yellow santolina and purple lavender billow forth in a mass planting.

Designing with Perennials and Annuals

Plant propagators are busy these days selecting new cultivars of old-fashioned perennials and annuals for homeowners to choose from. With so many plants available on the market, the challenge is how to begin to position them in your landscape.

Start with containers A good way to learn about effective plant combinations is to start by planting in containers. Try combining annuals, perennials, grasses, and even small shrubs or trees in planters that can range from small clay or plastic pots to cement or metal troughs. Starting from the middle, set tall, spiky plants like ornamental grasses just off center, surrounded by soft billows of perennials, and edged by low ground covers that hang down over the pot. You can even create a diminutive edible landscape of herbs, small fruits, or vegetables in pots and grow them on your deck or terrace.

Container gardening is a wonderful way to gain experience and confidence in designing with plants. These cascading plants complement the metal container, softening its strict geometry.

Plant in groupings Homeowners who are new to landscaping tend to buy just one or two of each kind of plant they're interested in. When planted alongside other single plants in a garden bed, what was beautiful as a specimen loses its impact. Instead, be bold and plant in large swaths of the same plant or in odd-numbered groupings of threes, fives, sevens, or more to ensure a natural irregularity to the grouping. A group of at least three plants together can be pruned as one billow, clump, or cluster. I like to repeat groupings like these several times in a garden to balance the blooming periods and leaf texture and color throughout the year.

It also pays to locate high plants in the back of the border and shorter plants in the front. This creates a kind of visual banking of plants that enables each to receive appropriate sunlight and airflow around their root systems. Using a mix of evergreen and deciduous materials in the same bed keeps it looking green throughout the winter when the deciduous plants have lost their leaves.

Mulching Using an organic mulch around your plants offers many advantages. Bark mulch adds a blanket around the stems of your plants, reduces evaporation, and helps hold in water. It can also reduce the spread of disease and give your planting beds a finished look.

Avoid the temptation to overmulch, which is a common failing in yards across America. For many people, once the mulch layer is installed, the landscape feels complete until it is renewed the following year. For me, mulch is a means of holding down weeds and keeping moisture in the soil until my plantings can take hold and grow in, not a ground cover in and of itself. In fact, too much mulch over a period of years can actually induce nitrogen deficiency in your plants.

When you do use mulch, look for the darkest color with the smallest-size particles possible. Mulch that has been composted for a year or more before being spread is often the best because it most resembles garden soil and looks as though it belongs there. Darker colors also set off the plantings and define the edge of the beds. Bright

EDGE BENEFITS

When you keep the edges of your planting beds sharp and neat, it gives your whole landscape a lift by clearly separating the garden area from the lawn. You can use steel edging, bricks on edge, or cobblestones, but the least expensive solution is to cut a simple spaded edge. First, define the bed line using a flat-edged shovel or a spade, making a 3-in. vertical cut. Then make another cut at a 45-degree angle toward the planting bed, removing all extra soil. It's an easy way to keep your borders looking trim—and much more natural than using plastic edging.

Tall poles strung for beans stand out in the middle of this home vegetable garden.

Here are some simple rules for making a successful vegetable garden:

- **Select a site in full sunlight that's not too far from your kitchen door for ease of access.**

- **Vegetables that produce fruit like tomatoes must be grown in full sun; leafy vegetables such as spinach or cabbage can be grown in partial shade.**

- **Make sure the plot has fertile, well-drained soil that's free of stones.**

- **Work in well-composted organic matter to improve the soil, using a trowel, spading fork, or a rotary garden tiller, depending upon the size of the plot.**

- **Make sure you have access to a nearby water source and give the garden a good soaking at least once a week, or install drip irrigation throughout your beds.**

- **After each rainfall, cultivate the garden to keep down the growth of weeds. Using mulches such as straw, hay, or grass clippings helps control weed growth while preserving moisture.**

red hemlock mulch stands out too much in a landscape, and large nuggets overwhelm the more delicate plantings they are covering. A rule of thumb is to use about 2 in. of well-composted mulch around your plantings the first year after installation.

Vegetable Gardening

For many people, nothing gives more pleasure than growing their own herbs and vegetables, whether in raised beds, containers, or a fenced-in garden. And with the rising costs of food and transportation and concern about the overuse of chemicals in agriculture, there's a resurgence of interest in growing one's own food. The success of a vegetable garden involves attracting pollinators—birds, bees, and butterflies—so plant a mix of perennials and shrubs around your vegetables that delight your senses as well. Design in a bit of shade for yourself by placing a bench under an ornamental tree at the end of the garden. And don't forget to plant seeds with your children and watch the thrill in their eyes as the seedlings grow.

Water in the Landscape

Like earth, water is an essential element and one that can provide unique opportunities for sensory pleasure in the home outside. Water in the landscape takes many forms, but they can essentially be reduced to two broad categories: still water and moving water. Still water, whether in a pool or a pond, has its own unique appeal, whether serenely calm or reflecting everything around or above it. Moving water—in a stream, a waterfall, or a spray jet in a fountain—holds our attention with its dynamic qualities.

Brightly colored cold-water fish bring life to a still backyard pond. These koi fish (Japanese carp) can grow as long as 3 ft., so they need a good-size pond to swim in.

(far left top) Water, stones, and plants combine to animate a corner of this tiny courtyard, where plants cascade from metal "window boxes" mounted on the wall.

(far left bottom) Rain chains, which function as open-air downspouts, are a unique way to bring the pleasures of moving water to your home landscape. The water weaves through the decorative links and can be collected in large barrels. In winter, the water freezes solid in a silvery ribbon.

(left) Installing an outdoor shower at a sheltered corner of your property brings its own kind of pleasure: immersion while surrounded by plantings.

Look for opportunities to introduce water features such as small ponds, artificial streams, and water basins that are visible from both inside and outside your house. Consider locating a water feature to signal a pausing place along a path, or installing a rill—a little stream or brook—to energize the flow within the landscape. Especially in hot and dry climates, where the sound and sight of a fountain or pool cools the atmosphere, water delights, soothes, and sustains us all.

Fire: Thermal Delight

To many people, there's nothing more magical than being outside in a warm place looking up at a cold night sky. Hardy folk erect a tent in the snow and enjoy winter camping. The rest of us prefer our creature comforts, so look to outdoor fireplaces, fire pits, bake ovens, grills, and even new propane heaters on stands to turn the cold into an asset.

DID YOU KNOW?

In the dry months of summer, you can save water and money and help recharge aquifers by harvesting rainwater in a barrel. Since rain is naturally soft water, you can use it directly on your garden—your plants will love it.

Nothing's better than firing up a gas grill on a cold winter's night and cooking up some hamburgers, grilling some veggies, or steaming some fish in foil. Yet most people forget that they own a grill once summer's over. Locating it close to the kitchen door under cover of a porch roof keeps the elements out, but mine is on our open deck and I grill in snow and rainstorms and in the coldest temperatures. Charcoal grills and smokers also work throughout the year, letting us prepare meals outdoors no matter what the weather.

Outdoor fireplaces offer a central hearth and focal point for family gatherings and parties throughout the year. Use their solid stone or masonry structure to extend the house outward onto the landscape. By combining a fireplace with an outdoor kitchen or grill and a durable living and dining room set, you'll create a home outside that meets your every need and allows kids to grill marshmallows throughout the year.

An old woodstove doesn't have to be hooked up to create a cozy corner in a fenced-in backyard.

Fire pits are another draw that brings people together outside at all times of year. These days, fire pits come in all sizes and shapes, from decorative metal stands to *chimineas* (Mexican fireplaces) to the simple holes in the ground. Some are moveable, others permanent.

If you can afford one, an outdoor hot tub or sauna gives thermal delight throughout the seasons, in every kind of weather. While the idea of the hot tub perched at a remote spot on your property is very romantic, the truth is that you want to be able to get to it efficiently from inside. In northern climes, you'll need to shovel snow away from the tub before you can jump in, so keep the journey from inside to tub as short as possible. Make the path to the tub easily traversable and easily shoveled. Put out hooks for robes or towels, a place for flip-flops or other light footwear, and some low lights for finding the tub on the darkest nights. Orient the tub to a distant view; if possible, place it looking out onto water to get the relationship of water to water.

Lighting for Ambiance and Safety

When I was 11, my family moved to a wonderful old house with two outdoor patios aptly named the White Terrace and the Black Terrace. The White Terrace stretched along the back of our house, with a view onto a formal boxwood garden. It had white, wrought-iron furniture set out on bluestone pavers. Lit from inside the house and with a few spotlights in the garden, it was a wonderful place for festive parties and alfresco dinners under the stars.

But the Black Terrace was my favorite because the lighting was more understated and mysterious. It was set at the edge of the garden, surrounded by a sitting wall of brick topped with bluestone, and it overlooked a sunken lawn. We'd sprawl out there in black-painted metal lounge chairs during many a hot summer night. Centered on a massive maple tree, the terrace came alive with leafy shadows cast by down lights set high, creating a remote place that expanded the pleasures of the garden.

(above left) Much like an indoor fireplace, a *chiminea,* or outdoor wood-burning stove, is built with a chimney or neck that controls drafts and protects the fire from sudden gusts of wind. Traditional *chimineas* from Mexico are built of clay; newer models are made of cast iron or cast aluminum that lasts for many years.

(above center) An inexpensive portable fire pit is all it takes to bring thermal delight into your home outside. Make sure to check with your local fire marshall regarding local fire-pit regulations.

(above right) Moonlighting casts light down from on high, often through trees, to create a subdued, romantic, and more natural effect, whereas uplighting, as the name suggests, casts light from the ground upward onto an object.

SIMULATE YOUR LIGHTING SCHEME

A good way to visualize how lights might look around your property is to place flashlights, candles, luminaria, or kerosene lamps in key locations to simulate a lighting scheme. Set out your faux lights at twilight on a cloudy day and play with their effects in the dark. Try the same lighting scheme on a night when the moon is full and see what changes. The only problem with this idea is that your garden may look so beautiful with candlelight that you may never want to install permanent lighting.

Finding interesting and imaginative ways to light your property is another way to find thermal delight in your home outside. Artful lighting enhances a property's beauty, while functional lighting makes pathways and steps safer and a backyard feel more secure. Outdoor lighting can expand a home's living space to outdoor social areas. Illuminating architectural features, sculpture, great specimen trees, or sculptural plantings creates drama in your backyard.

To begin conceptualizing a lighting plan, walk around your property at night, looking at it with fresh eyes. Imagine coming home on a dark, moonless night. You'll want to have a well-lit place to park and subtle but safe path lights that lead you from your driveway to your doorway. You might want to highlight the elegant weeping tree in the corner of the front yard. If you have a garden path that leads to the back, that should be lit, too. In the backyard, sconce lights attached to the house can light up a deck or terrace, while floodlights at the eaves can offer security lighting, when needed, for the whole backyard.

For special events like weddings, you can light up your garden using candles or small votive lanterns on long sticks that look like fireflies in the landscape.

Arts and Crafts-style lanterns sit on low stone piers to light the steps and signal the location of landings.

OUTDOOR LIGHTING

Thoughtful placement of lighting around high-traffic areas enhances your outdoor experience and makes walkways safe. Here, a single spotlight highlights an important tree that becomes a focal point in the dark.

Air: Breathing in the Out-of-Doors

One of the greatest sensory pleasures to enjoy in the home outside is the simplest one of all: breathing in fresh air. Feeling the cool of the evening's air on our skin, tasting snowflakes on our tongue during a winter's snowstorm, smelling the newly wet soil in the garden after a spring shower, or basking in the morning sunlight on a summer's day—these are all the atmospheric delights that we take for granted but that affect every aspect of our well-being in our home outside.

Wind chimes, mobiles, flags, and wind vanes all let us know of what is happening in the air around us. That same wind dries our clothes on the line—giving them a fresh scent while saving energy to boot. The more time we breathe in the out-of-doors, the more we're reminded to protect what we love.

Sensory pleasures abound in the out-of-doors. By extending the presence of home outside to the very edges of your property, you create the conditions for greater happiness in your life and that of your family. When you move outside the four walls of your house to become a part of the natural world once more, you are able to set aside your everyday stresses and contemplate what it means to be a part of the universe.

ENERGY-EFFICIENT OUTDOOR LIGHTING

Artificial lighting consumes almost 15 percent of a household's electricity use. If you use new lighting technologies, you can reduce the use of lighting energy in your home by more than 50 percent. Here are some basic ways to achieve more energy-efficient outdoor lighting:

- Remember, landscape lighting does not always need to be bright to be effective.

- If you use incandescent lights, make sure they are on a motion detector or a timer so that they stay on only as long as they are needed. Otherwise, use photo sensors with fluorescent or low-pressure sodium lights since they are much more energy efficient than incandescents.

- To reduce light pollution, use covers, deflectors, or reflectors on outdoor light fixtures. This will also help to make more efficient use of the light source. Again, use timers and other controls to turn decorative lighting on and off.

- It pays to use outdoor solar lighting where possible, although some areas of the country are too cloudy for this option.

Strands of hanging glass rings animate a landscape in more ways than one. They veil the garden, rotate in the wind, and scatter shards of light while making a gentle crystalline sound.

A CALIFORNIA PLEASURE GROUND

Large houses on small lots require creative design solutions, especially when you live in California where you can be outside year-round. This Mediterranean home near Sacramento had already received a total landscape renovation when landscape designer Michelle Helzer bought it. The bones of the landscape were good: a side pool, stucco retaining walls, and full drainage and irrigation systems. What it lacked were defined, usable outdoor spaces and a touch of pizzazz. Michelle set out to provide them.

First, she cut down the ugly strip of concrete to make a pathway of geometric stepping stones, which she stained a muted terra-cotta color. To tie new elements to the existing pool tiles, she used cobalt blue on the shed wall, as the color for pots and containers, and in the recycled glass "mulch" between the stepping stones. For good drainage, Michelle made a decomposed granite dining patio, lining the existing raised bed with hedges for privacy. U-shaped arbors of raw steel were built on both ends of the dining space and

connected with airline cable from which is suspended a dazzling Moroccan chandelier. The table can accommodate up to 18 for alfresco dining.

In the end, Michelle was able to separate and define the narrow lot into different living spaces, just like the inside of a house. With a living room, bar room (loggia), dining room, utility room (shed), lounge, and bathing room (pool and spa), this garden is truly a home outside.

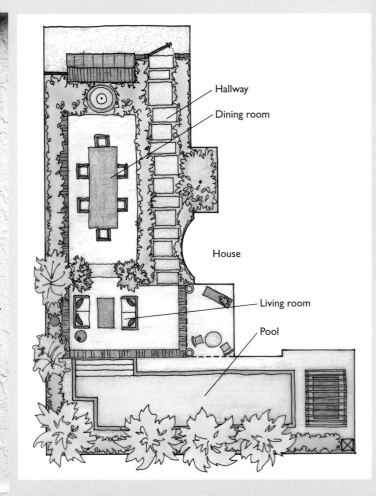

Hallway

Dining room

House

Living room

Pool

¹ A "hallway" of recycled concrete cut into pavers links the various "rooms" to each other.

² A quirky assortment of personal items, including a decorative parasol, grace a handsome wooden sideboard used for outdoor buffets.

1 A Buddha statue stands guard over the "living room" next to the pool. 2 A small swimming pool adds the element of water to this intimate garden full of sensory pleasures.

3 The hot colors of cannas, datura, agave, and orange bird-of-paradise are just a few of the exotic plants in the garden.

4 A Moroccan lantern purchased at a flea market is suspended over the hallway.

5 A chandelier of colorful votives and candles on "thrones" light a festive dining table.

Afterword: A Cottage in the Woods

Throughout this book, we've looked at a range of homes that illustrate specific principles of landscape design. To conclude, I'd like to focus on one modest property that shows how *all* the concepts can work together. It will serve both as an example of one person's journey through the design process and as a summary of the entire book. As you'll see, the owner of this house was able—over time—to transform a nondescript landscape into his own true pleasure ground.

Landscape architect Nick Cavaliere found his dream home 10 years ago in a 1930s summer community called Cedarcroft in Brick, New Jersey. Originally built as seasonal cottages for weekend getaways, many of these bungalows have been winterized for the homeowners who live there full time.

Lay of the Land

You'll recall that the first thing to do as you consider the lay of the land is to assess the actual site. Nick did just that. When he first saw this charming Craftsman-style house, it had been badly neglected, but all the original character and details were still intact. The landscape was equally derelict. The previous owners had rented the house for 17 years, and no landscaping had been done at all. For the first several years, Nick restored the inside of the 675-sq.-ft. house, which contained the original cedar paneling, stone fireplace, and a secret staircase to the basement hidden in a window seat. Once the interior was complete, he turned his talents to the outside.

Nick thought carefully about the elements of his ideal site. He grew up in the Pine Barrens of New Jersey, where he'd been interested in gardening from early childhood, taking care of his parents' property and working at a perennial nursery as a teenager. During college, he spent two summers abroad studying landscape ar-

(above) When Nick first saw the house, it sat on a barren front yard.

(left) This quaint bungalow blends beautifully into its landscape thanks to the homeowner's care in matching planting hues to paint colors.

A photo that Nick took on a trip to Europe inspired him as he developed the landscape around his house.

chitecture in France and Germany, discovering the joys of *Kleingartens*—"little gardens" that were small plots of land like community gardens, only with tiny cottages on them. These landscapes served as the inspiration for his own property where he sought to create a little weekend getaway zone surrounded by beautiful gardens.

When Nick took our Designer's Personality Test (see pp. 40–41), he came out as expressive, principled, practical, and orderly. His aesthetic preferences (see pp. 44–45) are: formal, asymmetrical, filled up, social, vertical, light, curved, flat, and intimate. Each of these traits fits his home outside perfectly, except for one characteristic: light. Nick wishes he had more sun-filled areas, but with those tall oaks, he's learned to live with shade.

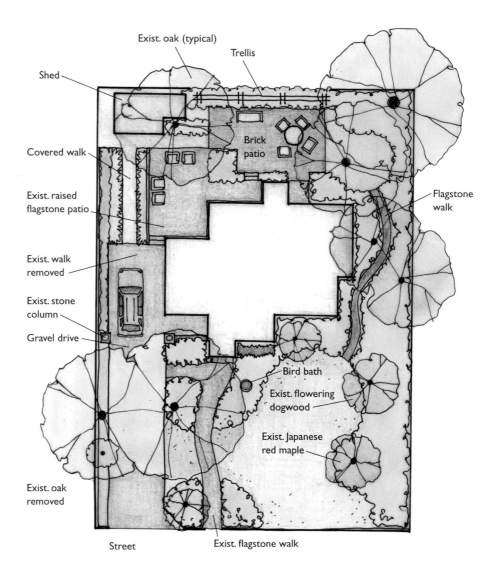

Big Moves

Nick decided that he wanted to keep a traditional House Front and Center layout for his small property that measures only 60 ft. by 80 ft. deep. He chose to arrange much of the site as Voluptuous Curves, except for the area between house and shed, where he used an All Lined Up arrangement to work with the existing raised flagstone patio. As for identifying a theme, Nick's Big Idea was to create a "woodland cottage," that is, a whimsical landscape with fun details at every turn. Many visitors tell him that he's created a Hansel and Gretel cottage or a Shire cottage from *Lord of the Rings*.

Nick was only 27 years old when he bought the property, and he had to stretch to be able to afford it. He couldn't accomplish everything at once, so he added things as he could, little by little. He did create a Master Plan—or "game plan" as he calls it—something he believes even the smallest property needs, since space is so critical. To this day, he continues to add things that he thought of when he developed his plan eight years ago.

Because Nick wanted to draw attention to his charming cottage, he chose House Front and Center as one of the Big Moves for the property.

Comfort Zones

The *Surrounding Zone* of this area is rich in local history. Native Indians named the river the property sits on the Metedeconk, meaning "beautiful wide river." Since it is surrounded by water on three sides, Cedarcroft's tagline is "where the forest meets the shore." With its old-growth vegetation, proximity to water, and narrow, winding roads that preserve existing trees while slowing traffic, the community also serves as a popular bird sanctuary.

Overwhelmed by the original driveway that took up much of the front yard, the Welcoming Zone was anything but. Nick decided to relocate the driveway to the side lot line, aligning it with two existing stone columns. This move allowed him to plant on either side of the front walkway, which made the driveway and cars less conspicuous. He replaced the original rusty old lamppost and mailbox with one that sits on a wooden post with a vintage 1920s light fixture.

(above) A period metal glider sits up against the wooden arbor, creating a handsome Living Zone in this narrow backyard.

(left) Mortared flagstones make a colorful patio for outdoor entertaining.

In such a tight community, creating enclosures at just the right locations was important for getting the Neighboring Zone right. First, Nick moved a dozen overgrown rhododendrons that were screening the foundation and nearly covering the house to the side yard as an instant screen. He installed a cedar fence along the driveway side, layered with a privet hedge. He also built a shed, with details to match the house, so that it blocks the view of his neighbor's deck and preserves a big white oak tree. Since the rear yard is so narrow (only 16 ft. deep) he needed to make the most of the space. Rather than planting large evergreens along the back, he chose to build a trellis with wisteria planted at the base of each column. Over time, the vines will weave together and form a visual barrier between properties.

Making the most of the Living Zone space meant that Nick decided to keep an existing raised flagstone patio just off the back of the house intact. Because of the dense shade and so little room, he decided to brick over his backyard instead of installing lawn, giving him a no-maintenance space for gathering. He created small lawn areas as play zones for his dog.

(below left) A mailbox is a piece of architecture, too. Nick brought the details of his house right out to the street in making a lamppost that doubles as a mailbox.

(below top right) Nick moved some old rhododendrons from the front of the house to the side lot line to create a living enclosure there.

(below bottom right) On the other side, a newly installed cedar fence brings privacy to the close-knit backyards. At the back corner, a new shed is a mini-version of the house.

(right) Not only an effective focal point but also a useful storage space for garden tools, this tiny shed adds a lot of charm to Nick's property.

(facing page) With so many containers to fill, Nick enjoys having a potting table close at hand in his garden.

Flow

Except for moving the driveway, Nick wanted to keep the original flow around the property much as it was. The curving flagstone walkway in the front offered an interesting "path to follow" from street to front door. He reused flagstones from the old driveway to create both paths and "places to pause" to encourage visitors to come around back. Rather than using impervious asphalt for the driveway, he chose a ⅜-in. red crushed gravel instead, a color that complements the colors of the house. He carried this gravel as a narrow, canal-like path alongside the flagstone patio with the charming shed as a physical and visual destination.

Nick also thought carefully about the shape of the lawn areas, designing them as sweeping curves to create pools of space, both in the front and back yards. When the front walk crosses the lawn, it feels like a bridge over water, pooling to become a turning point where it joins the short path that connects driveway to front walk.

Placing the Pieces

Nick was well aware that the most important focal point on his property was the house itself. When he bought it, all the trim and special detailing had been painted the same color as the body of the house. He spent nearly two years sanding it back to the wood and repainting it in a shade of olive green and sage, cream, and red—the complement to green. The result, according to his neighbors, is inspiring.

(left) A birdbath rests in the middle of billows of plantings: red impatiens, lime green hakonechloa, and large-leafed hosta.

(far left) Toadstool sculptures set in a planting of ferns and hostas draw the eye, despite their diminutive size.

The second most important focal point was his shed. With its location close to the house and on axis with the driveway and street, passersby enjoyed a clear view to the new building. Rather than buying a prefabricated shed, he bartered his landscape services with his carpenter neighbor and created an inexpensive but effective mini-version of the house. At the rear of the shed he stores two 12-ft. kayaks. Having found an old door and leaded-glass window at a salvage yard, he designed the shed around them—focal points within a focal point. With its diminutive size and charming details, it looks like a dollhouse, the envy of all the little girls in the neighborhood.

Nick placed smaller focal points that were both functional and aesthetic. Building on the area's renown as a bird sanctuary, he set a birdbath in the front yard, made from a 100-year-old mold. He found a matching birdhouse while on a trip to the Adirondacks and painted it to match the colors of the house. An old wooden cart from a local junkyard sits filled with flowers at the edge of the side yard.

Sensory Pleasures

As well as being a talented designer, Nick is also a consummate plantsman. Again, given the size of his site, he needed to be selective about what trees to plant. He planted a compact dogwood in the front yard as an under story to the massive oak trees and a handsome birch tree in a corner to the right of the front door to balance the two decorative high gables. He chose a warm color scheme for his shrubs and perennials, based on the palette of colors on his house and selected for shade tolerance. Despite the small size of the property, his plantings include 17 types of shrubs, 30 varieties of perennials, 9 different hostas, and 11 varieties of spring flowering bulbs. Planted in billows and layers, these plantings beautifully echo the color of the house and theme of the property. The parts feel like a living piece of the whole.

Nick also places 35 pots and hanging baskets to augment color and textures around the living areas of his home outside. Ever resourceful, Nick turned an old workbench that he found in the basement into a potting shed. His choice of furnishings is in keeping with the style of the house and has sentimental value: his great-aunt owned the old metal glider.

Nick feels very lucky. His home, both inside and outside, is the perfect size for his active lifestyle. His lawn can be cut in less than two minutes and the front yard watered by one sprinkler. Now that the garden is established and needs less care, he can sit back and enjoy a well-deserved rest.

Nick's dog sits at a "place to pause" along the stepping-stone side path to the back terrace.

Credits

p. 2: Photo © Allan Mandell, Design: Julie Moir Messervy Design Studio

p. 3: Photo © Randy O'Rourke, Design: Maggie Judycki, GreenThemes Inc.

p. 4: (left) Photo courtesy Virginia Hand; (right) Photo © Jacqueline Koch, Design: Leslie Howell

p. 5: Photo © Randy O'Rourke, Design: Salsbury-Schweyer, Inc.

Chapter 1

p. 6: Photo © Genevieve Russell, Design: Donna Bone, Design with Nature

p. 7: Photo © Charles McCulloch, Design: Charles McCulloch

p. 8: (left) Photo © Genevieve Russell, Design: Donna Bone, Design with Nature; (right) Photo © Nicola Browne, Design: Piet Oudolf

p. 9: (left) Photo © Alex MacLean; (right) Photo © Ken Gutmaker, Design: Ross Chapin, Ross Chapin Architects

p. 10: Photos courtesy MJ McCabe Garden Design, Design: MJ McCabe Garden Design

p. 11: (left) Photo © Randy O'Rourke, Design: Anya Zmudzka Sattler, ArtGarden Design; (right) Photo © Randy O'Rourke, Design: Salsbury-Schweyer, Inc.

p. 12: Photo © Nicola Browne, Design: Dan Pearson

p. 13: (top) Photo © Charles Mayer, Design: SE Group; (bottom) Photo © Randy O'Rourke, Design: Julie Moir Messervy Design Studio

p. 14: (top) Photo © Randy O'Rourke, Design: Maggie Judycki, GreenThemes Inc.; (bottom) Photo courtesy Chux Landscaping, Design: Chux Landscaping

p. 15: (top) Photo: Julie Siegel, Design by Julie Siegel; (bottom) Photo: Nick Cavaliere, Design: Nick Cavaliere

p. 16: (top) Photo © Dave Barnett, Design: Julie Moir Messervy Design Studio; (bottom left) Photo courtesy Myke Hodgins, Hodgins and Associates Landscape Architects, Design: Myke Hodgins, Hodgins and Associates Landscape Architects; (bottom right) Photo courtesy EyeCandy Marketing & Design, Design: Michelle Helzer, Lotus Designs Inc.

p. 17: (top) Photo © Randy O'Rourke, Design: Alice Moir; (bottom) Photo © Ketti Kupper Art & Design Inc., Design: Ketti Kupper Art & Design Inc.

p. 18: (left) Photo © Jan Enright; (right) Photo © Virginia Weiler, Design: Jan Enright, Jan Enright and Associates Landscape Design

p. 19: Photos © Virginia Weiler, Design: Jan Enright, Jan Enright and Associates Landscape Design

Chapter 2

p. 20: Photo © Randy O'Rourke, Design: Broadleaf Landscape Architecture

p. 21: Photo © Charles Mayer, Design: SE Group

p. 22: Photo courtesy Chux Landscaping, Design: Chux Landscaping

p. 23: Photo courtesy Cynthia Knauf, Design Cynthia Knauf Landscape Design

p. 24: Photo courtesy Broadleaf Landscaping Architecture

p. 25: (left): Photo © Genevieve Russell, Design: Donna Bone, Design with Nature; (right) Photo courtesy Myke Hodgins, Hodgins and Associates Landscape Architects, Design: Myke Hodgins, Hodgins and Associates Landscape Architects

p. 26: Photo courtesy Lynda Goddard; Design: Lynda Goddard, Gordon Ratcliffe Landscape Architects

p. 27: Photo courtesy Ron Rule; Design: Ron Rule

p. 28: Photos courtesy Salsbury-Schweyer, Inc., Design: Salsbury-Schweyer, Inc.

p. 29: (left) Photo © Genevieve Russell, Design: Donna Bone, Design with Nature; (right) Photo © Nicola Browne, Design: Laure Quonium

p. 30: Photo © Genevieve Russell, Design: Donna Bone, Design with Nature

p. 31: (left) Photo © Rosemary Fletcher, Design: Derby Farm Flowers and Gardens; (right) Photo © Allan Mandell, Design: Stacie Crooks

p. 32: Photo courtesy Myke Hodgins, Hodgins and Associates Landscape Architects

p. 33: Photo © Allan Mandell

p. 34: (left) Photo courtesy Broadleaf Landscape Architecture, Design: Broadleaf Landscape Architecture; (right) Photo © Randy O'Rourke, Design: Broadleaf Landscape Architecture

p. 35: (left) Photo courtesy Broadleaf Landscape Architecture, Design: Broadleaf Landscape Architecture; (right) Photo © Randy O'Rourke, Design: Broadleaf Landscape Architecture

pp. 36–37: Photos © Randy O'Rourke, Design: Broadleaf Landscape Architecture

p. 38: (top left) Photo courtesy Myke Hodgins, Hodgins and Associates Landscape Architects, Design: Myke Hodgins, Hodgins and Associates Landscape Architects; (top right) Photo © Randy O'Rourke, Design: Anya Zmudzka Sattler, ArtGarden Design; (bottom) Photo © Allan Mandell

p. 39: Photo © Randy O'Rourke, Design: Broadleaf Landscape Architecture

p. 40: (left) Photo © Randy O'Rourke, Design: Maggie Judycki, GreenThemes, Inc.; (left center) Photo © Nicola Browne, Design: Stephanie Grimshaw and Steve Leon; (center right) Photo © Randy O'Rourke, Design: Broadleaf Landscape Architecture; (right) Photo © Nicola Browne, Design: Bettina Bulaitis

p. 41: (left) Photo © Ken Gutmaker, Design: Ross Chapin, Ross Chapin Architects; (left center) Photo © Randy O'Rourke, Design: Salsbury-Schweyer, Inc.; (right center) Photo © Nicola Browne, Design: Kristof Swinnen; (right) Photo © Laura Broderick, Design: Laura Broderick

p. 42: (top) Photo courtesy Julie Moir Messervy; (bottom) Photo courtesy Charles McCulloch, Design: Charles McCulloch

p. 43: (left) Photo courtesy Paul Wieczoreck Design, Champlain Valley Landscaping; (right) Photo © Randy O'Rourke, Design: Broadleaf Landscape Architecture

p. 44: (top left) Photo © Nicola Browne, Design: Piet Oudolf; (top right) Photo © Ketti Kupper Art & Design Inc., Design: Ketti Kupper Art & Design Inc.; (center far left) Photo courtesy MJ McCabe Garden Design, Design: MJ McCabe Garden Design; (center left) Photo © Genevieve Russell, Design: Donna Bone, Design with Nature; (center right) Photo: © Steve Gunther, Design: Mia Lehrer & Associates; (center far right) Photo courtesy Salsbury-Schweyer, Inc., Design: Salsbury-Schweyer, Inc.; (bottom far left) Photo courtesy Cynthia Knauf, Design: Cynthia Knauf Landscape Design, Inc.; (bottom left) Photo © Genevieve Russell, Design: Donna Bone, Design with Nature; (bottom right) Photo courtesy Ron Rule, Design: Ron Rule; (bottom far right) Photo © Charles Mayer, Design: SE Group

p. 45: (top far left) Photo © Randy O'Rourke, Design: Alice Moir; (top left) Photo courtesy Fauteux and Associates, Design: Fauteux and Associates; (top right) Photo courtesy Little & Reid, Innovative Gardens, Design: Little & Reid, Innovative Gardens; (top far right): Photo © Nicola Browne, Design: Craig Bergmann; (center far left) Photo © Randy O'Rourke, Design: Salsbury-Schweyer, Inc.; (center left) Photo © Charles Mayer, Design: SE Group; (center right) Photo © Randy O'Rourke, Design: Salsbury-Schweyer, Inc.; (center far right) Photo © Nicola Browne, Design: Trudy Crerar; (bottom left) Photo © Nicola Browne, Design: Dan Pearson; (bottom right) Photo courtesy Holly Alderman, Design: Mary Lord

p. 46: (left) Photo © Randy O'Rourke; (right) Photo © Randy O'Rourke, Design: Maggie Judycki, GreenThemes, Inc.

p. 47: (top left) Photo © Randy O'Rourke, Design: Maggie Judycki, GreenThemes, Inc.; (top right) Photo © Allan Mandell, Design: Julie Moir Messervy Design Studio; (bottom left) Photo courtesy Victoria Lister Carley, Design Victoria Lister Carley; (bottom center) Photo © Randy O'Rourke, Design: Maggie Judycki, GreenThemes, Inc.; (bottom right & right center) Photos courtesy Myke Hodgins, Hodgins and Associates Landscape Architects, Design: Myke Hodgins, Hodgins and Associates Landscape Architects

p. 48: (left) Photo courtesy Mia Lehrer & Associates, Design: Mia Lehrer & Associates; (right) Photo © Steve Gunther, Design: Mia Lehrer & Associates

p. 49: Photos © Steve Gunther, Design: Mia Lehrer & Associates

Chapter 3

p. 50: Photo courtesy Ted Baker, Baker Turner Inc., Design: Ted Baker, Baker Turner Inc.

p. 51: Photo courtesy Myke Hodgins, Hodgins and Associates Landscape Architects, Design: Myke Hodgins, Hodgins and Associates Landscape Architects

p. 52: Photo © Nicola Browne, Design: Neil Diboll

p. 53: (left) Photo © Randy O'Rourke, Design: Salsbury-Schweyer, Inc.; (right) Photo © Charles Mayer, Design: SE Group

p. 54: (left) Photo © Randy O'Rourke, Design: Judith Reeve Landscape Design; (right) Photo © Rosemary Fletcher, Design: J&D Landscape Contractors

p. 55: (left) Photo © Randy O'Rourke, Design: Anya Zmudzka Sattler, ArtGarden Design; (right) Photo courtesy Chux Landscaping, Design: Chux Landscaping

p. 56: Photos courtesy Chux Landscaping, Design: Chux Landscaping

p. 57: (left) Photo © Roy Grogan, Design: John Szczepaniak Landscape Architect; (right) Photo courtesy Mary Dewart, Dewart Design, Design: Mary Dewart, Dewart Design

p. 58: (left) Photo courtesy Broadleaf Landscape Architecture; (right) Photo © Randy O'Rourke, Design: Broadleaf Landscape Architecture

pp. 59–61: Photos © Randy O'Rourke, Design: Broadleaf Landscape Architecture

p. 62: (left) Photo courtesy Myke Hodgins, Hodgins and Associates Landscape Architects, Design: Myke Hodgins, Hodgins and Associates Landscape Architects; (right) Photo © Nicola Browne

p. 63: (left) Photo © Nicola Browne, Design: Ross Palmer; (right) Photo © Nicola Browne, Design: Julie Moir Messervy Design Studio

p. 64: Photo © Nicola Browne, Design: Kristof Swinnen

p. 65: (left) Photo courtesy MJ McCabe Garden Design, Design: MJ McCabe Garden Design; (right) Photo © Randy O'Rourke, Design: Salsbury-Schweyer, Inc.

p. 66: Photos © Nicola Browne, Design: Piet Oudolf

p. 67: Photo © Steve Gunther, Design: Mia Lehrer & Associates

p. 68: Photo © Ken Gutmaker, Design: Alma Hecht, Second Nature Design

p. 69: (left) Photo © Nicola Browne, Design: Julie Moir Messervy Design Studio; (right) Photo © Nicola Browne, Design: John Brookes

p. 70: Photo courtesy Bethany Gracia

p. 71: (top left) Photo © Allan Mandell, Design: Stacie Crooks; (top right) Photo © Tim Ireland, Design: Christie Dustman, Christie Dustman and Company, Inc.; (bottom right) Photo © Nicola Browne, Design: Trudy Crerar

p. 72: (left) Photo © Nick Cavaliere, Design: Nick Cavaliere; (right) Photo © Nicola Browne, Design: Evan English

p. 73: (left) Photo courtesy Susan Parrish Carter, Gnome Landscapes, Design and Masonry Design: Susan Parrish Carter, Gnome Landscapes, Design and Masonry; (right) Photo © Genevieve Russell, Design: Donna Bone, Design with Nature

p. 74: Photo © Ken Gutmaker, Design: Ross Chapin, Ross Chapin Architects

p. 75: (top) Photo courtesy Alma Hecht, Second Nature Design, Design: Alma Hecht, Second Nature Design; (bottom) Photo © Randy O'Rourke, Design: Broadleaf Landscape Architecture

p. 76: Photo © Allan Mandell, Design: Alice Moir

p. 77: (left & top right) Photos © Allan Mandell, Design: Alice Moir; (bottom right) Photo © Randy O'Rourke, Design: Julie Moir Messervy Design Studio

pp. 80–83: Photos © Ken Gutmaker, Design: Alma Hecht, Second Nature Design

Chapter 4

p. 84: Photo © Randy O'Rourke, Design: Salsbury-Schweyer, Inc.

p. 85: Photo courtesy Real Eguchi, Eguchi Associates Landscape Architects, Design: Real Eguchi, Eguchi Associates Landscape Architects

p. 86: (top left) Photo courtesy Sharon Slocum, Inspired by Nature; (bottom left) Photo courtesy Myke Hodgins, Hodgins and Associates Landscape Architects, Design: Myke Hodgins, Hodgins and Associates Landscape Architects; (bottom right) Photo © Randy O'Rourke, Design: Anya Zmudzka Sattler, ArtGarden Design

p. 87: Photo courtesy Paul Wieczoreck Design, Champlain Valley Landscaping

p. 88: (left) Photo © Randy O'Rourke; (right) Photo courtesy Alma Hecht, Second Nature Design, Design: Alma Hecht, Second Nature Design

p. 89: Photo © Charles Mayer, Design: SE Group

p. 90: (left) Photo © Allan Mandell, Design: Lily Maxwell; (right) Photo © Steve Gunther, Design: Mia Lehrer & Associates

p. 91: Photo © Ken Gutmaker, Design: Ross Chapin, Ross Chapin Architects

p. 92: Photo © Kim Stuart, Design: Ron Rule

p. 93: Photo courtesy Myke Hodgins, Hodgins and Associates Landscape Architects, Design: Myke Hodgins, Hodgins and Associates Landscape Architects

p. 94: (left) Photo © Randy O'Rourke; (right) Photo courtesy Christie Dustman, Christie Dustman and Company, Inc., Design: Christie Dustman, Christie Dustman and Company, Inc.

p. 95: Photos © Randy O'Rourke, Design: Salsbury-Schweyer, Inc.

p. 96: Photos courtesy Mary Dewart, Dewart Design, Design: Mary Dewart, Dewart Design

p. 97: (top) Photos © Randy O'Rourke, Design: Maggie Judycki, GreenThemes, Inc.; (bottom) Photo © Randy O'Rourke, Design: Anya Zmudzka Sattler, ArtGarden Design

p. 98: Photo © Genevieve Russell, Design: Donna Bone, Design with Nature

p. 99: Photo © Randy O'Rourke, Design: Alice Moir

p. 100: (photo 1) Photo © Randy O'Rourke, Design: Maggie Judycki, GreenThemes, Inc.; (photo 2) Photo courtesy Lyne Legault; (photo 3) Photo © Randy O'Rourke, Design: Salsbury-Schweyer, Inc.; (photo 4) Photo © Tim Ireland, Design: Christie Dustman, Christie Dustman and Company, Inc.; (photo 5) Photo courtesy Arthur Lierman Landscape Architect, Design: Arthur Lierman Landscape Architect

p. 101: (photo 6) Photo courtesy Christie Dustman, Christie Dustman and Company, Inc., Design: Christie Dustman, Christie Dustman and Company, Inc.; (photo 7) Photo © Allan Mandell, Design: Birgit Piskor; (photo 8) Photo © Ken Gutmaker, Design: Alma Hecht, Second Nature Design; (photo 9) Photo © Allan Mandell

p. 102: Photo © Randy O'Rourke, Design: Leslie Howell

p. 103: (top) Photo courtesy Victoria Drakeford, Design: Victoria Drakeford; (bottom left) Photo © Randy O'Rourke; (bottom right) Photo courtesy Nick Cavaliere, Design: Nick Cavaliere

p. 104: Photo © Randy O'Rourke, Design: Alice Moir

p. 105: Photo © Ken Gutmaker, Design: Ketti Kupper Art & Design, Inc.

p. 106: (left) Photo courtesy Chux Landscaping, Design: Chux Landscaping; (right) Photo © Ken Gutmaker, Design: Ross Chapin, Ross Chapin Architects

p. 107: Photo courtesy Jordan Honeyman Landscape Architecture, Design: Jordan Honeyman Landscape Architecture

p. 108: Photos courtesy Bob Jonas; Design: Julie Moir Messervy Design Studio

p. 109: (top) Photo © Ken Gutmaker, Design: Ross Chapin, Ross Chapin Architects; (bottom left) Photo courtesy MJ McCabe Garden Design, Design: MJ McCabe Garden Design; (bottom right) Photo © Ken Gutmaker, Design: Ross Chapin, Ross Chapin Architects

p. 110: Photo © Nicola Browne, Design: Judy and David Drew

p. 111: (top left & bottom) Photos courtesy Mary Dewart, Dewart Design; (top right) Photo © Ken Gutmaker, Design: Donna Bone, Design with Nature

pp. 112–13: Photos © Randy O'Rourke, Design: Maggie Judycki, GreenThemes, Inc.

p. 114: Photo © Genevieve Russell, Design: Donna Bone, Design with Nature

p. 115: (top) Photo © Randy O'Rourke, Design: Anya Zmudzka Sattler, ArtGarden Design; (bottom left) Photo © Randy O'Rourke, Design: Salsbury-Schweyer, Inc.; (bottom right) Photo courtesy Victoria Lister Carley, Design: Victoria Lister Carley

p. 116: Photo © Ken Gutmaker, Design: Alma Hecht, Second Nature Design

p. 117: (left) Photo © Ken Gutmaker, Design: Ross Chapin, Ross Chapin Architects; (right) Photo courtesy Charles McCulloch, Design: Charles McCulloch

p. 118: (photo 1) Photo © Ken Gutmaker, Design: Ross Chapin, Ross Chapin Architects; (photo 2) Photo courtesy David Powell, Design: David Powell; (photo 3) Photo © Tim Ireland, Design: Christie Dustman, Christie Dustman and Company, Inc.

p. 119: (photo 4) Photo courtesy Little & Reid, Innovative Gardens, Design: Little & Reid, Innovative Gardens; (photo 5) Photo © Nicola Browne, Design: Judy and David Drew; (photo 6) Photo courtesy Victoria Drakeford, Design: Victoria Drakeford;

(photo 7) Photo courtesy Real Eguchi, Eguchi Associates Landscape Architects, Design: Real Eguchi, Eguchi Associates Landscape Architects; (photo 8) Photo courtesy Arthur Lierman Landscape Architect, Design: Arthur Lierman Landscape Architect

p. 120: Photo courtesy Myke Hodgins, Hodgins and Associates Landscape Architects, Design: Myke Hodgins, Hodgins and Associates Landscape Architects

p. 121: Photo © Rosemary Fletcher, Design: Koletta Kaspar, A Yard and A Half

pp. 122–125: Photos © Ken Gutmaker, Design: Todd Paul, Architect: Ross Chapin, Ross Chapin Architects

p. 126: (top) Photo courtesy Victoria Lister Carley, Design: Victoria Lister Carley; (bottom) Photo courtesy Chux Landscaping, Design: Chux Landscaping

p. 127: Photo © Randy O'Rourke, Design: Julie Moir Messervy Design Studio

p. 128: Photo © Randy O'Rourke

p. 129: Photo courtesy Real Eguchi, Eguchi Associates Landscape Architects, Design: Real Eguchi, Eguchi Associates Landscape Architects

p. 130: Photo courtesy Victoria Lister Carley, Design: Victoria Lister Carley

p. 131: (top) Photo © Randy O'Rourke, Design: Julie Moir Messervy and Steve Jonas; (bottom) Photo © Randy O'Rourke, Design: Salsbury-Schweyer, Inc.

p. 132: Photos courtesy © Alma Hecht, Second Nature Design, Design: Alma Hecht, Second Nature Design

p. 133: Photo courtesy Jordan Honeyman Landscape Architecture, Design: Jordan Honeyman Landscape Architecture

p. 134: Photo courtesy Victoria Lister Carley, Design: Victoria Lister Carley

p. 135: (top & bottom right) Photo courtesy Myke Hodgins, Hodgins and Associates Landscape Architects, Design: Myke Hodgins, Hodgins and Associates Landscape Architects; (bottom left) Photo © Randy O'Rourke, Design: Alice Moir

p. 136: Photo courtesy Mary Dewart, Dewart Design

p. 137: (left) Photo © Rosemary Fletcher, Design: Reed Hilderbrand Associates, Inc.; (right) Photo © Allan Mandell, Design: Laura Crockett

p. 138: (left) Photo © Randy O'Rourke, Design: Julie Moir Messervy Design Studio; (right) Photo © Nicola Browne, Design: Blackenham Wood

p. 139: (top left) Photo © Randy O'Rourke, Design: Salsbury-Schweyer, Inc.; (top right) Photo courtesy Real Eguchi, Eguchi Associates Landscape Architects, Design: Real Eguchi, Eguchi Associates Landscape Architects; (bottom) Photo courtesy Sharon Slocum, Inspired by Nature, Design: Sharon Slocum, Inspired by Nature

Chapter 5

p. 140: Photo © Randy O'Rourke, Design: Anya Zmudzka Sattler, ArtGarden Design

pp. 141–142: Photos courtesy Virginia Weiler, Design: Jan Enright, Jan Enright and Associates Landscape Design

p. 143: (left) Photo courtesy Salsbury-Schweyer, Inc., Design: Salsbury-Schweyer, Inc.; (center) Photo

© Allan Mandell; (right) Photo © Charles Mayer, Design: SE Group

p. 144: (left) Photo © Randy O'Rourke, Design: Salsbury-Schweyer, Inc.; (right) Photo © Randy O'Rourke, Design: Anya Zmudzka Sattler, ArtGarden Design

p. 145: Photo © Randy O'Rourke, Design: Salsbury-Schweyer, Inc.

p. 146: (left) Photo courtesy Anya Zmudzka Sattler, ArtGarden; (right) Photo © Randy O'Rourke, Design: Anya Zmudzka Sattler, ArtGarden Design

p. 147: Photos © Randy O'Rourke, Design: Anya Zmudzka Sattler, ArtGarden Design

p. 148: (left) Photo © Nicola Browne, Design: Bettina Bulaitis; (right) Photo: © Randy O'Rourke, Design: Maggie Judycki, GreenThemes, Inc.

p. 149: Photo © Randy O'Rourke, Design: Broadleaf Landscape Architecture

p. 150: (left) Photo © Allan Mandell, Design: Laura Crockett; (right) Photo courtesy Jordan Honeyman Landscape Architecture, Design: Jordan Honeyman Landscape Architecture

p. 151: (left) Photo courtesy Dave Barnett, Design: Julie Moir Messervy Design Studio; (right) Photo © Nicola Browne, Design: Daniel Ost

p. 152: (left) Photo courtesy Suzanne Edney, Design: Suzanne Edney, Suzanne Edney Custom Landscapes; (right) Photo: © Randy O'Rourke, Design: Maggie Judycki, GreenThemes, Inc.

p. 153: (top) Photo courtesy Holly Alderman, Design: Holly Alderman; (bottom left) Photo © Randy O'Rourke, Design: Maggie Judycki, GreenThemes, Inc.; (bottom right) Photo © Randy O'Rourke, Design: Salsbury-Schweyer, Inc.

p. 154: (left) Photo courtesy Chux Landscaping, Design: Chux Landscaping; (right) Photo: © Randy O'Rourke, Design: Anya Zmudzka Sattler, ArtGarden Design

p. 155: Photo © Randy O'Rourke

p. 156: (top left) Photo © Randy O'Rourke, Design: Julie Moir Messervy Design Studio; (top right) Photo © Randy O'Rourke, Design: Salsbury-Schweyer, Inc.; (bottom) Photo © Genevieve Russell, Design: Donna Bone, Design with Nature

p. 157: (left) Photo © Ken Gutmaker, Design: Ketti Kupper Art & Design, Inc.; (right) Photo © Grey Crawford, Design: Julie Moir Messervy Design Studio

pp. 158–59: Photos courtesy Virginia Weiler, Design: Jan Enright, Jan Enright and Associates Landscape Design

p. 160: (top) Photo courtesy Arthur Lierman Landscape Architect, Design: Arthur Lierman Landscape Architect; (bottom) Photo courtesy Myke Hodgins, Hodgins and Associates Landscape Architects, Design: Myke Hodgins, Hodgins and Associates Landscape Architects

p. 161: (left) Photo courtesy Real Eguchi, Eguchi Associates Landscape Architects, Design: Virginia Burt, Visionscapes Landscape Architects; (right) Photo courtesy MJ McCabe Garden Design, Design: MJ McCabe Garden Design

p. 162: (left) Photo: © Genevieve Russell, Design: Donna Bone, Design with Nature; (right) Photo

© Randy O'Rourke, Design: Maggie Judycki, GreenThemes, Inc.

p. 163: (left) Photo © Nicola Browne, Design: John Brookes; (right) Photo © Nicola Browne, Design: Isabelle Greene

p. 164: (left) Photo courtesy Arthur Lierman Landscape Architect, Design: Arthur Lierman Landscape Architect; (right) Photo © Genevieve Russell, Design: Donna Bone, Design with Nature

p. 165: (left) Photo courtesy Holly Alderman, Design: Holly Alderman; (right) Photo courtesy MJ McCabe Garden Design, Design: MJ McCabe Garden Design

p. 166: (photo 1) Photo © Allan Mandell, Design: Alma Hecht, Second Nature Design; (photo 2) Photo courtesy Virginia Weiler; (photo 3) Photo courtesy Myke Hodgins, Hodgins and Associates Landscape Architects; (photo 4) Photo courtesy Victoria Drakeford, Design: Victoria Drakeford; (photo 5) Photo © Tim Ireland, Design: Christie Dustman, Christie Dustman and Company, Inc.

p. 167: (photo 6) Photo © Nicola Browne; (photo 7) Photo courtesy John Szczepaniak Landscape Architect, Design: John Szczepaniak Landscape Architect; (photo 8) Photo © Randy O'Rourke, Design: Broadleaf Architecture

Chapter 6

p. 168: Photo © Randy O'Rourke, Design: Broadleaf Landscape Architecture

p. 169: Photo courtesy Virginia Weiler

p. 170: (top) Photo courtesy Salsbury-Schweyer, Inc., Design: Salsbury-Schweyer, Inc.; (bottom left) Photo courtesy EyeCandy Marketing and Design, Design: Michelle Helzer, Lotus Designs, Inc.; (bottom right) Photo © Genevieve Russell, Design: Donna Bone, Design with Nature

p. 171: Photo courtesy Ron Rule Consultants, Design: Ron Rule Consultants

p. 172: Photo © Genevieve Russell, Design: Donna Bone, Design with Nature

p. 173: (left) Photo © Genevieve Russell, Donna Bone, Design with Nature; (right) Photo © Randy O'Rourke, Design: Broadleaf Landscape Architecture

p. 174: (left) Photo © Genevieve Russell, Design: Donna Bone, Design with Nature; (right) Photo © Randy O'Rourke, Design: Maggie Judycki, GreenThemes, Inc.

p. 175: Photo © Randy O'Rourke, Design: Alice Moir

p. 176: (photo 1) Photo © Ken Gutmaker, Design: Alma Hecht, Second Nature Design; (photo 2) Photo © Randy O'Rourke, Design: Maggie Judycki, GreenThemes, Inc.; (photos 3, 4, and 6) Photo © Randy O'Rourke, Design: Julie Moir Messervy Design Studio; (photo 5) Photo © Allan Mandell, Design: Victoria Lister Carley

p. 177: (photo 7) Photo © Randy O'Rourke, Design: Maggie Judycki, GreenThemes, Inc.; (photo 8) Photo © Allan Mandell, Design: Birgit Piskor; (photo 9) Photo © Allan Mandell, Design: Stacie Crooks

p. 178: (top) Photo © Dency Kane, Design: Julie Moir Messervy Design Studio; (bottom left) Photo © Randy O'Rourke, Design: Leslie Howell; (bottom right) Photo © Randy O'Rourke, Design: Julie Moir Messervy Design Studio

p. 179: (top) Photo courtesy Laura Broderick, courtesy Laura Broderick; (bottom left) Photo courtesy Sharon Slocum, Inspired by Nature, Design: Sharon Slocum, Inspired by Nature; (bottom right) Photo © Nicola Browne, Design: Piet Oudolf

p. 180: Photo © Dency Kane, Design: Julie Moir Messervy Design Studio

p. 181: (left) Photo © Genevieve Russell, Design: Donna Bone, Design with Nature; (right) Photo © Randy O'Rourke, Design: Salsbury-Schweyer, Inc.

p. 182: (left) Photo courtesy Ketti Kupper Art & Design, Design: Ketti Kupper Art & Design; (right) Photo © Ken Gutmaker, Design: Ketti Kupper Art & Design

pp. 183–85: Photos © Ken Gutmaker, Design: Ketti Kupper Art & Design

p. 186: (left) Photo courtesy Virginia Weiler, Design: Jan Enright, Jan Enright and Associates Landscape Design; (right) Photo courtesy EyeCandy Marketing and Design, Design: Michelle Helzer, Lotus Designs, Inc.

p. 187: (left): Photo © Ken Gutmaker, Design: Ketti Kupper Art & Design; (right) Photo courtesy Lyne Legault

p. 188: Photo courtesy Julie Moir Messervy

p. 189: (left) Photo courtesy Julie Moir Messervy; (right) Photo © Randy O'Rourke, Design: Salsbury-Schweyer, Inc.

p. 190: (left) Photo courtesy Ashley Ford, Design: Ketti Kupper Art & Design; (right) Photo © Genevieve Russell, Design: Donna Bone, Design with Nature

p. 191: (left) Photo © Randy O'Rourke, Design: Julie Moir Messervy Design Studio; (right) Photo courtesy Julie Moir Messervy

p. 192: (left) Photo © Jeannie Sargent, Design: Broadleaf Landscape Architecture; (right) Photo © Steve Jonas, Design: Julie Moir Messervy Design Studio

p. 193: Photo © Randy O'Rourke

p. 194: (bottom) Photo courtesy Maggie Judycki, GreenThemes, Inc., Design: Maggie Judycki, GreenThemes, Inc.; (center and top) Photos © Randy O'Rourke, Design: Maggie Judycki, GreenThemes, Inc.

p. 195: (left) Photo © Randy O'Rourke; (top right) Photo © Allan Mandell, Design: Alice Moir; (bottom right) Photo © Randy O'Rourke, Design: Maggie Judycki, GreenThemes, Inc.

p. 196: Photo © Nicola Browne, Design: Daniel Ost

p. 197: (left) Photo © Randy O'Rourke; (right) Photo © Nicola Browne, Design: Bettina Bulaitis

p. 198: Photo © Nicola Browne

p. 199: (left) Photo courtesy Holly Alderman, Design: Holly Alderman; (right) Photo © Nicola Browne

pp. 200–203 Photos: © Randy O'Rourke, Design: Julie Moir Messervy Design Studio

Chapter 7

p. 204: Photo © Genevieve Russell

p. 205: Photo © Virginia Weiler

p. 206: Photo courtesy MJ McCabe Garden Design, Design: MJ McCabe Garden Design

p. 207: (top) Photo © Genevieve Russell, Design: Donna Bone, Design with Nature; (bottom left) Photo courtesy Holly Alderman, Design: Holly Alderman; (bottom right) Photo courtesy Maggie Judycki, GreenThemes, Inc., Design: Maggie Judycki, GreenThemes, Inc.

p. 208: (left) Photo: courtesy Leslie Howell, Design: Leslie Howell; (right) Photo: courtesy Chux Landscaping, Design: Chux Landscaping

p. 209: Photo: © Nicola Browne

p. 210: (photos 1 and 3) Photo courtesy MJ McCabe Garden Design, Design: MJ McCabe Garden Design; (photo 2) Photo courtesy Ted Baker, Baker Turner Inc., Design: Ted Baker, Baker Turner Inc.; (photo 4) Photo © Allan Mandell, Design: Birgit Piskor

p. 211: (photos 5 and 6) Photo courtesy MJ McCabe Garden Design, Design: MJ McCabe Garden Design; (photo 7) Photo © Allan Mandell, Design: Stacie Crooks; (photo 8) Photo courtesy Mary Dewart, Dewart Design, Design: Mary Dewart, Dewart Design

p. 212: Photo © Nicola Browne

p. 213: Photo courtesy Ted Baker, Baker Turner Inc.

p. 214: Photo © Nicola Browne, Design: Isabelle Greene

p. 215: (left) Photo courtesy Broadleaf Landscape Architecture, Design: Broadleaf Landscape Architecture; (right) Photo © Randy O'Rourke

p. 216: Photo © Allan Mandell, Design: Buell Steelman & Rebecca Sams

p. 217: Photo © Allan Mandell, Design: Jack Hagenaars & Keith Webb

p. 218: (left) Photo courtesy Salsbury-Schweyer, Inc., Design: Salsbury-Schweyer, Inc.; (right) Photo © Randy O'Rourke, Design: Salsbury-Schweyer, Inc.

p. 219: Photo © Randy O'Rourke, Design: Salsbury-Schweyer, Inc.

p. 220: (top) Photo © Genevieve Russell, Design: Donna Bone, Design with Nature; (bottom) Photo © Nicola Browne, Design: Jinny Blom

p. 221: (left) Photo © Randy O'Rourke, Design: Broadleaf Landscape Architecture; (right) Photo courtesy Jeffrey Mayes, Design: Mamie Wytral

p. 222: Photo © Randy O'Rourke, Design: Maggie Judycki, GreenThemes, Inc.

p. 223: (top left) Photo © Ken Gutmaker, Design: Ketti Kupper; (bottom left) Photo courtesy Virginia Burt, Visionscapes Landscape Architects, Design: Virginia Burt, Visionscapes Landscape Architects; (right) Photo © Nicola Browne

p. 224: Photo courtesy Victoria Drakeford

p. 225: (left) Photo © Ken Gutmaker, Design: Art & Design; (center) Photo courtesy Alma Hecht, Second Nature Design; Design: Alma Hecht, Second Nature Design; (right) Photo courtesy EyeCandy Marketing and Design, Design: Michelle Helzer, Lotus Designs, Inc.

p. 226: (left) Photo © Z Media, Design: Leslie Howell; (right) Photo courtesy Chux Landscaping, Design: Chux Landscaping

pp. 227–231: Photos courtesy EyeCandy Marketing and Design, Design: Michelle Helzer, Lotus Designs, Inc.

Afterword

pp. 233–41: Photos: courtesy Nick Cavaliere, Design: Nick Cavaliere

Index

Note: *Italicized* page numbers indicate that illustrations are included. (When only one number of a page range is *italicized,* illustrations appear on one or more of the pages.)